MW00528520

Boat

Boat

Lisa Robertson

Coach House Books, Toronto

copyright © Lisa Robertson, 2022

Earlier versions of some of these poems were published in *R's Boat* (University of California Press). This is the first edition of the complete manuscript.

Published with the generous assistance of the Canada Council for the Arts and the Ontario Arts Council. Coach House Books also acknowledges the support of the Government of Canada through the Canada Book Fund.

LIBRARY AND ARCHIVES CANADA CATALOGUING IN PUBLICATION

Title: Boat / Lisa Robertson.
Other titles: Poems. Selections
Names: Robertson, Lisa, author.
Description: Some poems were previously published in *R's Boat* (2010). Also contains previously unpublished poetry.
Identifiers: Canadiana (print) 20210353155 | Canadiana (ebook) 20210353171 | ISBN 9781552454404 (softcover) | ISBN 9781770567115 (PDF) | ISBN 9781770567108 (EPUB)
Subjects: LCGFT: Poetry.
Classification: LCC PS8585.O3217 R68 2022 | DDC C811/.54—dc23

Boat is available as an ebook: ISBN 978 1 77056 710 8 (EPUB); ISBN 978 1 77056 711 5 (PDF)

Purchase of the print version of this book entitles you to a free digital copy. To claim your ebook of this title, please email sales@chbooks.com with proof of purchase. (Coach House Books reserves the right to terminate the free digital download offer at any time.)

The ebb and flow of this water, its sound continuous but lapping with distances that ceaselessly caught up my ear and my eyes, replaced the interior emotions revery had quenched in me, and sufficed to make me pleasurably sense my existence without troubling to think.

– Jean-Jacques Rousseau

At the stage we've now reached, which is that of experimentation with new collective structures, with new syntheses, it is no longer the time to fight the values of the old world with Neo-Dadaist refusal. Whether those values are ideological, artistic, or even financial, we need to unleash inflation everywhere.

– Michèle Bernstein

Far before it communicates, language is for living.

– Émile Benveniste

CONTENTS

The Hut /

/ /

Day o   pens
an ovoid vase, an ov   oid vase with twisted
ribbing, an ovoid vase, green   green, clear, a slab, a shape
a cylinder, a   massy plaster
clo   ud
sun slips   upward
the one bodywid   e muscle speaks
I cross the room to w   alk toward a voice.

Voice, enteri   ng the city
sa   ys
because ther   e is no city
we make   things
if we can't usefully describe   artifice as transcendence
we'll die o   f money
and the realism   of constraint.
These ideas have nothi   ng to do with belief.

/ /

To separa   te belief
from the resin-scented plank   s of the cement housings
from tallish sha   ggy grasses
from masquerades, pro   cessions, allegories
from the elsewhere girl   s fuck in their lovers
I put myself o   utside thought
in fields of bleach   ed-out cornstalks
a bare tree   of apples
this is no   t a city
this perishab   le situation
the yellow band   of sky above it.

There's no formul a for the visible
it doesn't end. This is for
dogs, their serious ness and accuracy
for pig eons.

It's not far from morn ing and it's autumn.
Part of political li fe is not visible
at the core of th is a dissidence
its religiosity is structu ral rather than ideal.
I'm still you. Here we are.
This is my a ccount my
inward-open ing window
a flock of geese a herd of steer
share one bare field
by the Da isy-Mart.

Now all art i s impossible
that is its spe cial function
and also the c ompassion
for the political eco nomy of the future.
What would n't feel false?
Maybe those wildroses seen from the train will change what
the mi nd is.
Whatever mak es them speak
waves unde r wide light
the word rea lly is a prism
when I gather the se facts together
it is the work of the hands only.

I wanted to think into the structure of appearances
calling this 'anim al' 'body' 'heart'
but not in order to deplete them
I wanted to no te the passage

of cognitive perceptio   n into organic excitation
of organic excitation i   nto cognitive perception
of cognitive excitation   into organic perception
there was a time   when I came close
sometimes the heart   just nails you to a chair
I must speak   precisely now.

The serious mistakes – were   they mistakes in intention
or in em   phasis?
They are myths now an   d distant like myths
they def   ine me.
We're all pressed by urg   ent business as it were
out of this rise   s a question
What do w   e absent?
The quasi-m   ortal faun
whose thinking   is Phoenician?
We like to hide o   urselves behind
the gods w   e endure
and suddenly I'll   invoke anything
folder 10   track 20
at 14 minutes th   e sound of pages
turn   ing
a seal on a rock su   nning and twisting.

/ /

Because   we resist
there i   s spirit
it's a long h   istorical cry
across comple   x conditions
we hear our   ancestors
I call them o   ur ancestors
they're the on   es who insist

on watching d   awn starlings
the clouds are   puffy gold
striated by ele   ctrical lines
a dove calls i   n the village
in undulant m   odulations
I'm not for an   y betterment
the house is an ec   hoing instrument
I both receive for   m and invent it.

Any dawn invo   kes everything
everything to d   o with my body
because I   am a body
we must s   ense bodies
the existence   of our bodies
is not po   ssession
the situation of   sensing a body is
the beating of the heart in   the morning in the dark
before the   birds begin
is the sound of th   e heart breaking is
a female corpse   without identity
asleep at the   base of a tree
Psyche is the thou   ght that leaves her
clean as   a forest.

I would like a delicate   spring-flowering herb
a note   book
philosophy a   s housework.

Some were knowing   some were thinking
some were   making
they were undertaking their   research in places hidden or
unhi   dden
anywhere, beside r   ivers, beneath trees

in renovated basements, while browsing in chaotic junk shops
in attic libraries o f ship-like houses
on long flights on aeroplanes while sipping cheap cognac
while riding their bicycles to markets and gymnasia
gazing into the fog extremely early in the morning while the
radio fl ickered
sorting cutlery
some of their organs were outside history
this also me ant 'to think.'

The next idea – could pictures be heaven?
I go to the museum t o test the hypothesis
like anything having to do with my body
I'd like it to be lurid and light
rising and fall ing like an act
or the inestimable sp aciousness of trees.

Now I'm freely dreaming int o the sound of my heartbeat
if poetry i s to exist
it must say something
about surabu ndant ethics
with ferocio us humility
this could be my beginning
the desire to spe ak with the dog
from all the black m oods of the organs
near the public lilacs of the station lawn.

This would be ae sthetical I think.

/ /

Since I'm part of the aesth etic history of the ignorance
                    of L atin
I would like to be permit ted some whimsy as well.

A rare sap is flowing th rough the entire house
            lung-like and pronominal
        near the tree's l uxuriant sexes
What if I did assu me gods exist?
How would I con template them?
Someone opens a window I didn't know was there
            mainly there was shame
        and its portab le territory.

A day passes like a breath.
What will teach me how to die?
Tell me, sua ve diddling
rapacio us cupid
you who follow beginning's cord
to your feral pa rts, from which
slips a mi lky resin
feeding the world, ripping blandness from the chest
the ploughed-up districts palpitate
and I weep for d eath in general
and my body is th e image that weeps
I dress this bo dy against death
to dress is to have a soul
near the stillness o f closed wardrobes.

/ /

I remember the close ground, everything
growing from it
yellow wild snapdragon, Queen Anne's lace
milkweed, daisy, cornflower dandelion, timothy, burdock
I lay down in it with my own nerves and blood
I heard the ringing of my own nerves and blood
I was a falling star longing for the visible
hacked-off hair in 1995
Moby Dick Béla Tarr
I was the flexible medium of the future
and the impossibility of beginning
I was arching back to possess the sky
I was among rocks
longing for the visible.

Style is conflict.

Dear buggered-up style
I wake up sipping doubt
time holds the tree and I together
fog has held sound against the earth and muffled it
I burn like a candle
with the good luck to be born
It's a feeling that begins at my hip joints
and it radiates outwards
through the star of my body.

Is this the place where falling is made?
I have slept in its library.

Somethi ng bleats.
It really makes me want to w ear my feathered hip-skirt.

/ /

Everything I know about language
I learned from sex
I was really fuc ked up with fear.
You were really f ucked up with fear
so you stroked your own body.
She has a fl ower's throat
and listens with her eyes
the image rises in my thy mus like a beautiful smoke
clothing is landscape
fibre, drape, grief, labour
as well as soul
I went along in openness.
My pelvis and t he street spoke.

The men who can't father
because th eir fathers
broke them
they are o ur fathers.

/ /

August comes like wasps
don't b e lost
general chirpi ng of things
this world i s a donkey
with wicker w ings, very fine
golden and splend id and soon gone
for each revo lt, its apron

– 18 –

(refinement is   not a quality)
I could live in a hut with an an   imal and that would be god

To release o   ne's phantom
auto   nomy
gently into   the mouth
of the   lover
I have   a face.

/   /

Ricoeur, citing Benveniste: 'The sentence pours language
back into th   e universe.'
I think t   his is so
and if the se   ntence pours
it pours in   a direction.
Who pours t   he sentence?
The friend   pours it.

There's the p   ouring sense
the sentence as   this cup or vessel
or mouth, the mouthfeel o   f the sentence as it pours
near the long sighs   of the old radiator
we will protest, we will d   istinguish, we will laugh
there will sometimes be   long silences at tables
we will wonder abo   ut Zoroastrianism
I will wake up in the middle of   the night to tell you that I want
to be fe   arless.
'For you I want to be fe   arless' is the sentence.
We're full o   f secrets.
At 1 a.m. the sound of a snow   shovel's muffled scraping

Then once again I dis cover the feminine
annulled in some rare te xt I was about to idolize.
The feminine a gain needs me
or I need her anger
so as not to ag ain disappear.

/ /

Little Voice
surviv e then
whose H orizon
is an Ear

/ /

As for the ordinary femininity of the absolutely gratuitous
hori zon
the elsewhere of my gr andmother in my speech
or the little bone in the fo ot that Goethe discovered by
comparative deduction
I admire the o dd transitions
from frantic to stately
when my tongue sips her name
it goes, it carries, it b reaches, it sutures
smoothly the si gnalling sky
smoothly the bo ats on water
her forearm with t he awkwardness
at inner croo k of elbow
where lives
all the lost expressiveness i n the history of adolescence
pl us
the extraordinary mo bility and alertness
of horses viewe d from a train

it's still true that I want to decorate mortality
let's s tart.

There's no prob lem of influence
because everythin g in my life writes
even when I don't write
sometimes I say thing s I don't understand
I am in the landscape wh ich has aided my story
asleep in the sedu ctive landscape
I am leaning o n the railing
as a way of not b eing otherwise.

I wake up to the bellow ing of a cow through fog.
By rejecting the poets, he is expelling metaphor from
knowled ge because
metaphor can' t be legislated
whi le
Benveniste's poetics of linguisti cs is an opening to metaphor
to the temporal mo bility of the image.
Time is d ifficult.

In the vocal re volving night
the animal does n't have a soul
the animal is a soul
when I touch something I'm touching the culture of human
fin gers
which I believ e in strongly
I have a dou ble feeling
I'm strongl y grieving
when I wake into form I experiment with belief
I'm adding my own straw to contribute to the conflagration.

/ /

Big-dropped rain now knocking the yellow leaves from the field
ma ple
the intense thin gs in my mind
I'm afraid of them.
Duration is t he material.
It resi sts us.
There is the struggle betw een duration and the idea.
the rest is pebbles.
I just wait.

Where painting ends and medicine begins is a place
where a nearly total intimacy can ensue.
Karen cries on the bus.
There is an organ-like p roximity of documents
an animal is a u nit of attention
a truck passes, a dog bark s and then the frogs start
there is still the occ asional nightingale
style i s huge.

/ /

I was living in a hut on t he edge of fields as a form
of direct action.
No one re ally noticed.
Thinking in the hut is a refu sal of the quotidian as such.

Here I am thinking a bout time as negativity –
extinction, abol ishment, loss
but it is no t amusing.
The spleen's function, says Plato, is to keep the liver shiny
and spa rkling

then it can receive imag es as clearly as possible
upstairs, the husky scent of summer
all afternoon, sultry th under in the distance
the dog's dismay.

/ /

My right-side o vary spoke.

/ /

Maybe Venus is the spee ch of the image in thought.

Today, Sunday, 10:21 a.m. I am going for a feeling
the question of the origin of geometry will be that feeling
I am very uncomfortabl e and very stimulated.
As I write this I sweat.
Geometry brings the cae sura into any discourse
it is a port able gift
I can't say 'm y' caesura
as I can't say 'my' horizon
but they give me a stance.
Venus is a t ranscender
How did th at happen?
She stays on the surface.

With the flight path of a hornet I wrote
and then the voice said – m ust we oppose emotion to
philosophy and so on?
because subjectivity is the t ransformation of the social
and context's a synchrony beyond the object proper
all the novels I won't write a re passing through my hands
like w ater.

From prolixity   to parsimony
from hand   to water
the great sadness o   f incompleteness
the disrupte   d ordinary
these were the four th   ings I wanted to write
I spoke fro   m memory
a speaki   ng name.
Everything with the c   haracter of privacy
witne   sses
the branches of gr   ammar moving
the perplexing vernac   ular of wasting time.

.

A burst of rain, a bel   low of frogs, April
a dog, the hut, a sta   rry sky, a chimney
(the world has   a structure)
its meaning isn't twoness   but vibrant irregularity
it involves the fo   rm of speaking
sometimes unexpected   dly like a clear space
circumscribed   by mortality
sometimes at sea, someti   mes with a special herb
sometimes when   it is forbidden
on cus   hions

When it is forbidde   n there will still be
everything with the   character of money
which makes a state   ment seem authentic
but does s   o secretly.

Their link i   s arbitrary
but spea   king isn't.

Every secret divide s some institution
its detection is affecti ve, unspeakable, and so
another con cealment.

When we discove r a hidden thing
something else is hidden in its turn
and so on i nto history
This is what we call community.
It requires a silence t o produce perception.

/ /

Radiant wit h silent luck
those shapes which h ave been made precise
pour grace on a bare table
grace is to give g race to someone
In the inter est of grace
grace is certainly a part of painting
as well as o f medicine
when grace first came
it felt o bscure
like fated collaps es and mistakes
within the goo d use of silence
I lean into its mould.

It's 2 014
the year Coolidg e comes to Paris
I want the fa shion blogs
to speak p hilosophy
and still be the fashion blogs.

/ /

The ten-centim   etre handspan
is the unit of meas   ure of the present
there is less and less and the   body can disappear easily
there are   no pens
there have never bee   n pens in this world
we were never give   n the tool to do this
this present recor   d, this field work.

Now we have to in   vent the present
the present with i   ts mighty force
is sweatin   g all night
because it has   no place in life
the informati   on of our fear
is the pr   esent
is sweating   all night

The difference betwee   n pleasure and desire
is the result of a lesion t   he present is suffering
is looking for   a form of life

More perceiving   cries the present
into the infinity   of relationships.

/ /

When we flew over the green   illuminated game stadium
its scoreboa   rd blurred
by low   cloud
that was t   he cosmos.
Fjords, cloud   silver water
brid   ges

scrim of gold lig   ht and coolness
acts o   f lust
like eating the th   roats of thistles –
is there a way to   use everything?

The very difficulty of the con   cept caused a tactile pleasure in
my men   tal life.
I'm an athlet   e of solitude
within thi   s solitude
the same thing comes to   have a different meaning

I saw a don   key in a tent
I saw a farm wi   th both fires lit
I saw the da   rk and a spill
the articulation a   nd a moth in day
the difference between   a concept and a noun
is obs   olete?

/ /

What gets done wi   th what's obsolete?
what matters in the nar   rative is not the story
but the shad   ows it casts
narrative becom   es a linking space
where elements can be ta   ken up again, reanimated
it holds rather t   han represents
it's the storage sp   ace for concepts
like the night sky wi   th its constellations.

Debt has rep   laced Latin
As the univer   sal language.

/ /

The idea of the linguistically   unassignable is where I'll begin
this mo   rning
it's a late b   eginning
solitude is not the opposite of   sociality or the communal
it is sociality sl   owed down
to its most ineffici   ent manifestation
solitude is a techn   ique of slowness.

To me, spiritual expe   rience in airplanes
is part of a his   tory of retreat
in the plane   that night
everything bec   ame allegory
there is satisfact   ion in secrecy.

When grief change   d the colourfield
was grief a   hormone?
We watched night f   all on the subject
like a c   ocktail
and I thought I would like to lie   down in the dry leaves and fuck
and you rhyme hi   p-hop with Pope
in micro-units of e   nd-stopped sound
then the focus pul   ls back to the city
and I'm watching all the   full moons of Facebook
rising in digita   l increments.

Subjectivity i   s temporality
I read in   my notes.

/ /

There's no mystery to what　women do in history –
they think　by the fire.
Day after day I fail a　t what I have to do.
Alas, I forget – it's because th　e heart's torn out of my chest.
I go back to the idea of a　sonically installed irony.
I look up and the sky　is a vast pink palace
now ab　alone
now old indigo re　fracting silence.

Every soul is a k　not in rhythm.
What I want now is the quiet　ude of an internal resistance.
It has value only by　virtue of a history
and is total　ly arbitrary
which is to sa　y not natural
and is the on　ly continuity.

Between the fe　ast and the law
between epistemology and the　darkest organ of my pleasure
at times exaggerat　ed and withdrawn
I tho　ught
but with nothing so cru　de as an identification
I at least h　ad the right
to be free　as a man
as free as　a floating
trash　gyre
to fashion the co　mmunal material.
The dumbed-down material　ist is quite good for himself.
Gently I shed　my ambition.

// /

On a Thursday m   orning in April
I'm writin   g in bed
of the girl who dreamt of se   x in 1982 and took the train.
This problem of so   litude, what is it?
My imperative is to vai   ngloriously disbelieve
because the body is at every poi   nt a moving critique of history.
I speak to the d   og and tell her
this am   plitude
is the sub   jectivity
of rhy   thm.

By history I mean all these begi   nningless filaments of language
that intensify   in my organs
as the system   of my organs
also the experi   ence of loathing
and the impat   ient camera.

There must also be anger   in the descriptive project
such as the feeling of b   eing erotically assessed
by the powerf   ul aging man
who has beco   me potbellied.
Apart from   all of that
I would like some delicate   yet robust sonic shapes
calm and alert   and receiving.

It's by way of metaphor th   at the image enters the body
cellu   larly.

/ /

When I first noticed t he dust on the leaves, I
– adjectival, rinky-dink y, winsome – thought
must I ache?
To lie on a be d and scratch
to feel my clothin g against my skin
to gently rub my b are feet together
to rest my cheekbone on my opened-upward palm
there is no convinci ng etymology for it.
Jane Ellison says all se nsation is movement.
We want to know
how to let flesh be heard in our work.
Ordinary fero cities are nice.

The dry tree of the room is what the sun climbs.
My desire to admire
Humboldt, Bo pp, Saussure
was 2 010.

There were thi nking muscles
one's interes ting humility
the dream of th e body as a book
if I begin to write o n my own behalf
probably 'no fear' is not an option
neither is 'no belief'
at one and the same time we must philosophize, laugh, and
manage our household
says Ep icurus
and I sit in the material di versity of consciousness
and I leak.

In terms of medi cine or grammar
memory t ransmits
the smell of t he white page
and the vertical dimen sion of the green violet
I want to look at you a nd ask you questions
I google continuous movement and find
Thomas of Aquinas spea king of time and angels
in the *Summa* *Theologica*.

/ /

The soul *is* clinamen
I should r elax more
sociality is n't number
could philosoph y be a collage?
Simone We il says no
nor the relaxing equi valence of bodies.

I think a lot a bout death
why you died w hen you did
what came before
the frustrated love, days of exhilaration, defeat
whole pe oples die
the spiri t leaves
an emergenc y plants itself
calling my nam e in your voice
the perfume b ottle, 2/3 full
sits on the edge of the bedroom table
refracting t he 2011 sun.

/ /

Now for the pati ence of painting
now to construct P oussin indexically
in order to abolis h the distinction
between art and politics.

Firstly, the methodolog ical privacy of an idea.
I can only misun derstand death
but I feel it sen ds me images
standing enti rely aloof
there could be secrets I dedicat e myself to without knowing
what if my great long love is this foliage
I need to learn its materials.

/ /

Women of this stupid century
I feed you waln uts and whisky
and call i t georgic
now that I'm ad dressing you
I feel all bright.

The poem unwinds in excruc iatingly synthetic slow motion
before it acquires th e real time of reading
whatever that vari able may represent

In my experience it is not thro ugh identification but refusal
that the represe ntation is made
it must shed all elegance
against the vague hum of the heating apparatus
fleas move from bod y to body in the night
how is it that this perfectly predictable action suggests

that mind and matter ar e not separate systems?
All matter is abo ut to undo itself
by slowing down t he causal interval
without subjecting it to a s ubsequent recomposition

Here voice is not inst rument but topology
retaining all the sn ags and silliness
in the idea of the indexical.

/ /

Bronze, wax, inte rior shifting light
leaking from gaps b etween the planks
(perception i sn't retinal)
what if this index beco mes a mothering in me
that does n't stop?
What do I mother?

8 skulls found in a gard en in Perpignan in 2005
they extend unkn owably outwards

With secretive duration, the thickness of the senses, meaty
mort ality
and the total disr egard of decorum

Here I'm treating my mi nd's interior as a surface
because of the idea of a female latency
in the manifest o of lust in 1913
by Valentine d e Saint-Point.

Suddenly the horizon fell.
When did I bec ome Lucretian?
It was 2006

I was inclined to disidentify
to live at the dissolut ion of a designation
I could fail and this wo uld be a discipline also
and what I lo ved is flowers
and this is no t all I can do.

A girl c alls out
defiance, in sults, jeers
a girl whose styl e was breaking
I was t hat girl
outside the win dow is all frothy
even the tiny stick y leaves are frothy
the lilac buds a re black froth
this is the end of the notebook of 2006.

/ /

It was 2003
the beginning of the cata logue of the female pronoun
a fire had been burning. I wait.
The baroque wall clock wi th the base of hortensias
has stopped at eig ht minutes to ten.
A fax arrives f rom Jacques
(it is a Boul é horloge)
in the room sce nted with roses.
The story of the mauve For tuny gown, does it exist?
Money is a nervous sinew, a labyrinth, a delirium
painting is a hot, sweet, temp erate red humour moved by the
veins and the liver
its office is to give strength
to put belief and dissona nce together on a surface
like a layer of luxur ious silt that sinks.

Time in prose
becomes fearless
What I want to address here is inertia, sloth, and drag.
What can a sentence do besid es give more time to ideas?
the words become th e room of experience
as I w rite.

The horizontal quality of the shared project
resists the distinction between the essential and the accessory.
Could the poem revolve – as life
do es
and witn ess itself?
It is reasonab le to think so.
I can recognize myself in the ideological calm of these
anonymo us words.
It is the present and the hut em pties itself and the walls pull
ba ck
how could I feel so free?
at the edge of huge day
the stiff dress belling around my cold thighs
repose is unfinished and dependence is unfinished
and amongst this (timor mortis)
to resort to the here a nd now of atmosphere
like a lotion that flow s through all things.

/ /

To call my bio graphy *Errata*
might b e true
the sensation of ligh t is political maybe
as I leave the house
Agamben says all poetry is sub stitution and pain avoidance
then transcription be comes masquerade

the men I mimic
they trem ble in me
like a kiss commit ted to mortality
I have an emotion for transcription
what else is t here to do?
with neither preced ent nor antecedent
transcripti on is erotic.

I need a n ew erotics
a speech tha t writes itself
the clouds mim ic torn garments
Dresser's glass va ses seem to pour
my boots slip o n the cliff path
I continue a little way through broken snow
then think better of it
it is a disap pointment
I had wanted to stand like the moody hero of a German
Romantic painting
my greatcoat flapping i n the raw Atlantic wind
as I gazed at the cu rve of the horizon
in order to sustain the opacity of perception
this is an ordina ry catastrophe
and turning again to my notebook I write
It is 2004. Wha t shall I do?

One by one I recite plan ts, places, rivers, species
lis ten
where the pronoun swerves is freedom.

/ /

In 2 009
the inner swags of purple organ-life

elaborate the ner ves of discourse
this great, innocent manipulate d faith in the individual will is
not my t radition
but it is
is somet hing like
the soft nois e of fucking
the way it accomp anies the lateness
not of the body but of the polis
from the grubby punk tie-kn ot to the lacunary grammars
from the verb 'to be' to the semiotics of the animal
the capacity to destr oy and restructure
makes inexact repetitions as
the site ev aporates.

In the rare book room
with their 19 se xes on my sleeve
in a kind of shu nting migration
it gives me joy to be thorough
and yet
I want it to remain in human and obscure
I want to lie on my back in a cab in and look up at the rafters
listening to Bartó k on a cheap radio
I want also to go to a silent hotel
I want some objective photogr aphs of my unfamiliar body
I want to go spirituall y to the riverbank
I want to return to making sentences that go nowhere.

If I dared to execute t he prose of a female
without first imagining it and assigning this prose a style
this chair by the window
could be any s eat by any tree
I move deeper int o the apartment
or whatever para dise is made of.

/ /

The cabin with the wet bo ots at the door, paradise
the wood box full of wet woo d, the bark dust everywhere
para dise
and the kettl e on, paradise.
Was paradis e language?
The infinite pleasure of the ton gue on the palate is a paradise
I am saying that these phonemes can defend
whatever there is o f health in my cells
which will pertain eq ually to environments
or they will go down together
like everything incap able of measurement
the lyric is hereti cal secularism
metaphor makes subjects of us.

/ /

Morning soft and grey and as still as could be
it was winter and nothi ng resembled anything
I simply followed from wh ere I happened to begin
and then mov ed in a line
I could construct conversations
these conversations be came stages, or lungs
what if nature is subjectivity?
there is simply no tr ue determination
because language is a hormone –
it receives, it innovates, it trans forms, it engenders, it shows
the thread spinning subj ectivity from resistance.

The empty insecticide drums rusting under the rowan tree
the sound of thres hing at midnight
a coil of black plastic electric al tubing emerging from the

rubbl e heap
a warehouse fire in 1957
the black mould spores inhabiting the kitchen
an eddy of magp ies in January:
the drone of grief
bears all the marks of a n ordinary implausibility
mincing and lugubrious
intolerably s entimental
its weird intima cy and slippage
no middl e ground
no middle voice, Pete
there is nowh ere else to go.

I can't yet tell the difference b etween freedom and anarchy
what we ca ll a world
is not the oppos ite of anything
I still do n't know
I'm walking from w indow to window
watching the li ght on the field
scanning the s un in the tree
there's a solid t hread of water
joining bod y to body
where certain bodi es are elsewhere
what if this were not true, she asks
her voice a tre mulous velvet
the light changi ng every minute

I watched it from roo ms and cars and woods
disturbing flashes baroque sunbursts
buttoning and unbuttoning
then, from t ime to time
everything wr aps around us

rooms and car   s and woods
the truck on the horizon   flicks on its headlights.

/ /

I have two souls an   d one of them is fur
I have three souls and on   e of them swims in light
my extra souls   are earrings
laid out on a k   itchen table
in an apartment in Sa   n Francisco in 2005.
Another soul, the ultra-euph   oric swimmer in laughter
is her voice. S   he is a soul
she   says
I'm willing to say that we d   on't know anything even
about one g   rain of rice
against the dry h   acking of grief

Upstairs the wide planks, t   he motionless plenitude
hurled, falling and r   olling in mid-ether
for the vast eve   nt she swims in
the long lust of the 16   th stanza goes careening
in little pul   sing lights
and how n   ot to die.

Is my feeling   just too slow
beside the tree's   luxuriant sexes?
I let the fire burn down, m   y hand is cold on the pen
the dog whin   es as I write
using the instru   ment of my body
using the failu   re of emotion
a woman is eating roses and lil   acs, a shutter is pulled down
this work of idiocy, the figu   ring, this brawny doubt
I'm her   e for it.

The gestures in these roo ms expand and contract
like the red ball of the sun, 8:03 a.m.
now I want you to feed m e from your own mouth
like an animal or a mother
in order to relis h consequences
I assumed the ligh t was telepathic
though I didn't know how to interpret it.

I, leaking sal iva and revolt
stood on the por ch taking pictures
lay in the bath and breathed.
What living does to the body is i nteresting, ordinary and weak.

Then the cranes returne d, crying above the field.
A soul spo ke at 6 a.m.
it's not time to go to t he back of the night

So I will go to lo ok at paintings
here painting is wha t the land has made
it shows another way to be what we are
I have in my muscles a ki nd of all-purpose divinity
and the proliferative ina uthenticity of the concept
March 31 and I he ar the first cuckoo
and now the fro gs have started
Venus makes m e treasonous.

/ /

In 2 007
I am walking down the street getting sunburnt
I think of a sentence and it di sappears into the landscape
this movemen t is a pleasure
it is so arden tly cinema's

outmoded strenuous spiritual assertion
a pinky cloud-drift dispersed at 6:30 a.m.
I feel both humble and large.

There will be theories destined for salacious enjoyment
revelation in a series
theory as an aperture.
We carry the theories around with us until nothing is possible
I noticed it was words and I noticed they were women
perhaps breathing began as this radiant complicity.

We don't yet know how not to be hungry
this is the beginning of the ordinary
Gena Rowlands bowling in Lovestreams
is a placelessness where ancient revolutions slumber
she taught me a structure
did the rain stop falling? It did not
then lofty summer
I must drink more champagne.

/ /

The day is tinsel and scent
although I am most precociously patient
I can only bathe in the light and knit
one is no longer the potentially gorgeous womb
one is interdiction
philosophy feels possible
because of being interdiction

I wanted to know something about myself without it being
personal

- 43 -

I would knit and think and   I wanted it to never stop
the thread does n   ot always exist

If I write only with lo   ve and philosophy
with philosophy, whi   ch is love written
with fundamental cont   radiction which runs
like a red thread throug   h the whole of my life
a child in a red T-shirt walking   out across the lawn in summer
I feel myself become a   person in your gaze.

Over the space of 6–8 lines   flagrant syllabic pleasure
in the excellent   oblong codex
some pages damp   ened, some torn
one with a fingerprint of   ink in the lower margin
ink has splashed   the motile soul
and also the thread   y will in turmoil
(time being impossible   without the creature)

When we speak in t   he theatre of sex
we only ever des   cribe the state
the scale   is wrong
consent   retreats
the psychic feeli   ng is grammar.

/ /

To understand this grammar I   had to go outside a discipline
I still don't know   what language is
but nature here is the possib   le world, not the lost world.
Now begins a   manifesto:
a style cann   ot change
without changing th   e public of that style.
The weight of the book o   n my reclining pelvis

holds me   to earth.
Here I choose to work w   ith unstable materials.
Time enters the sente   nce as deterioration
there is the feeling of non-   permanence as a setting
the deep texture of   my body withdraws
I could feel fear tight   ening in my kidneys.

Sometimes I was recallin   g the library from the hut
and sometimes I was recall   ing the hut from the library.

It's heretical solitud   e I'm talking about –
I sit in the lib   rary and weep
the brittle flakes of ancient   paper and leather littering the
dark grey   broadloom
are the various hu   es of human skin
in conste   llation.
This is colo   nization.

A child explained the concept   of infinity to me whilst eating
grilled se   a bream
if knowledge i   s description
it satisfies, fee   ls, and drinks.

/ /

Did the questions co   me in prose or verse?
Were the questions prepared in   advance or formed on the spot?
Were they expressed in the s   tructure of two alternatives?
I ask them to cut the page   s of the two fascicles of the
Sogdia   n Sūtra
of Causes   and Effects
they are l   arge books
the sound of morning is the p   leasant song of the paperknife.

In what way is th e oracle inspired?
Did she requir e a translator?
Were the answers give n orally or in writing?
Were they precise and clear or enigmatic and ambiguous
as in lit erature?
What was the relation between aleatory consultation and
inspi ration?
Were these indep endent techniques
undertaken by s eperate personnel
or were they two levels, two mo vements, in the same practice?
These questions can't be answe red with complete assurance.
All of our intellectual co mposure is required.
The oracle is a craftsman.
The signs represented by smoke, by x-rays, by entrails
who will int erpret them?
An epistemological probl em is a political problem.

Yes. We are saying health is the refusal of the unification of the
body by an
epistemolo gical regime
in favour of an opening to a m aximally diverse expressivity.
In reality we slide through mo des of knowing continuously
our context – that of bein g among other bodies –
is so continuously op aque and variable
as to constitute a n environment
whose only constant is ong oing expressive mutability.
What is meant by intuition?
Sometimes analysis works, espe cially when supplemented with
conje cture.

To what extent can we conside r poetry as an epistemological
eve nt?
I said I wasn't sure. N ow I do feel certain

that the poem is a propositio n about the form of knowing
it is not a fault but a continuous form
a kind of path
that mus t be sung
before it d isappears.
Is an idea recogni zed or is it said?
Did the word *elli pse* exist as such?
Is it a sound or an event?
3 a.m. is a form. What a re your obligations?

/ /

It was a famou sly cold winter
the two absences – before and after
they fe lt true
to protect the charact er of the girl's desire
as the figure of a blazing
I'm deep in the obliterated region, dripping brightness.
How much life is stored in a vowel?
Older th an names
it l ies
and ex pires
successively the word s will be taken away
but the vowels will not be taken away
the smell of stale urine
at the heart of the rose is
vowel of the
communa l substrata.

Rimbaud has n ot quit poetry
She has quit the system of class.

She refused to re produce a class
instead she enters the infinity of linguistics
which i s what?
A solitary com mune in a hut.

She takes a bath
then dries her hair by th e fire as it snows outside
and the co ld leaks in.
This win ter only
her body escap es stratification
in favour of a spe ctacular physics
I exit the system of degradation
I close the n otebook
Rimbaud is n ot satisfied.

/ /

Here the trobar n otebooks begin.

The gorse bursts up yellow at the border of the woods
for 1000 years the continen t ceased to produce records
then came tre mbling spring
– they had inve nted spring –
a kind of pape ry palpitation
a literature of the body
whose communal tea rs flowed so sweetly
that if I am asked to think abou t something that does not exist
I can do s o readily.

Mystic boys wit h heads of mules
dolphins as non- human persons
what's the sweetest thi ng that can be said?
Because an imag e acts in bodies

with its   desire
on Apri   l the 4th
the frogso   ng starts.

Oh take off the fu   cking tight helmet
of thi   nking
for the total   imbrication
of ri   me
and shatter   ed gardens.

/ /

What if I begin with the di   verse and continue to move
toward th   e diverse?

there is p   leasure
in dis   tance
sa   ys
the nigh   tingale
whose   song
prod   uces
noth   ing
but sh   ows
and h   ides

Style is not proper to anyo   ne and neither is the refrain.
Once again I disag   ree with everything.
Me with my asym   metrical concepts
I know nothing o   f your interior life.

A neural ting   ling alerts me
to the presence o   f the hidden poem:
consciousne   ss is technical.

To rumpl   e or churn
to wave   or curl
to mitiga   te, abate
to chang   e course
often the visual is exp   erienced sonorously
love spills a   s a spindle
then s   tops
held by th   e thread
she herself h   as twisted.

The refrain is   communal
the door clicks o   pen on the night
and the dog goe   s into the yard
priva   tely:

The long winter of   politics is very dry
but sap   is wet
there were clea   r eyes, a forest
death will com   e, but not yet.

Sap i   s wet
Time   is wet
Love i   s wet
Grass   is wet
The guts and t   he heart are wet
Wet wi   th what
Total moral   abundance
All r   ight.

/ /

To show the lust of a girl or woman
truthful with endings, truthful with beginnings, truthful with
choosing

Fast beasts following rivers
green pectorals of mountains
little house of chopped-down fronds
to be ridden, submit to flowers
in skirt of mud
unsated, pull of seven skies
um, table it
tiny avid tummy
I bit a lad's attar
it's inimitable
I need, um, a generator, like some
cut, chilly Venus
like a horse's vigour
concealed prettily
ta-da! You take off on
adventure, yum
I bit something floral
I bit placating night
placidly in nighty
not some diddling nerve's quarrel with the ideal
not the ubiquitous terror of fructification

You want a big category?
I saw this bent I, a sign
beneath lippy sky
I had a strange but realistically forked feeling
about the things that weakened.

The problem is   a source of light.
I need a   library
many gravities, lin   king and rebounding.

/ /

There she is   (Rimbaud)
pacing in her revolut   ionary greatcoat
and midi   culottes.
What about sol   itude as an art
where all the elem   ents are invoked
with innumera   ble gradations
with reactions bot   h strong and weak?

What are we doing   with our bodies
why are   we here
who wore a little   feathered wing
in her   hair?

/ /

Sea of boats   earth of trees
bare sky of fol   ding language
each totally anima   te generation basks
confects   shivers
the sky inv   ents figures
should I d   rink beer
should I do the   green powders
should I count s   ervings of fruit
should I write longha   nd so as not to forget
what is s   adness
who ha   s died
how muc   h money?

The deep tire ruts in the grass   caused by the delivery trucks
are a   world
they are bri   nging books
I live in thos   e moist ruts.
I wasted the who   le night crying
going away from one lonel   iness and not toward it.
Once again I dedicated   myself to sensation.

/ /

That is how writing beca   me the story of my body
other bodies spoke in   the breaths of my body
they expanded benea   th my shoulder blades
in the long duration of my n   ext breath writing burned
on the surface   of my breasts
swimming into the ocean wh   ich is also a kind of writing
more and more I slip   ped under the surface
Even if   failing

The sheer   massiness
of wr   iting
is a force of   cohesion.
Then a quiet th   ought arrives
making me s   hyly happy
– at least my sad   ness is my own.

/ /

I walked through the waist-high   wheat and it flowed like green
wa   ter
I only want   ed to know
about love a   nd solitude
to receive the   m to the core

and I am so tired of the f urniture of psychology
cumbersome dark inherited things
smelling of dust
and futile ca lculation.

Next the scent of the rain arrives
and then the rain
and then the commu nications are undone
and dove s return
and the great e cstasy of sleep
in afte rnoon

All space is sy mbolic space
the plums drop into the swimming pool
I'm 52

Soft sweet cricket-buoyed m usk of earth as Venus rises
becaus e of this
I need a lot of solitude
figs hard on trees
and the desir e to be useless

/ /

Loved and l ost at once
togethe r when
to love is t o have lost
and to be lo st is to love
love's lost e ver limned
elemental love elemental loss
have to be together
at once limi nal and ever

/ /

Practice l oving now
a white butter fly floats past
I think of Mallarmé
psyche i s a book
the young girl gla ncing downwards
in the attitud e of reflection
she shows in her reflection
the strict geomet ry of her hair part
downwar d pointing
a horizo n rotated
it is a vertic al horizon
in the girl the hor izon has rotated
what wil l endure
in a s ign?

/ /

I wanted to experien ce form as duration
like a hairpin marking a page
like everything pure that I started in my long youth
all self-serious a nd heartbroken
the time I went crazy when my dog ran into the forest
for four days I walked thr ough wheatfields crying
the green wheat partin g below my breastbone
every butterfly tha t obliquely passed
was a girl in a dress
maybe reading is abo ut this vast desire for the
invi sible
my breath my hou se my twin my equal
my absolute conte mporary adored one

sometimes the sun vi   brates with a whirring
when I pass it   s open window.

/   /

New ho   urs open
my inexper   ienced style
they are soft   fresh hours
rare a   nd fresh
I'm alive so I can t   ell you these things
how we became an   d remained subjects
or per   fumes
and I wanted to flee   my great mistake
I do not c   are for it
nor the offic   ial violence.

I had an idea about t   ime while I was walking
it was that writi   ng displaces time
its setting is not   fully the present
writing d   efers time
the time of pron   ouns for example
is syn   thetic
between spea   ker and receiver
writing schemati   zes this between

I don't k   now you
and this is the ne   cessary synthesis
I'm not sure this is   so, but it could be
subjectivit   y is thrown
nothing has ever   occurred before
yet i   t has
what a relief t   o be weeping
what an od   d passion.

/ /

The poets wh o have died
they say we should tak e advantage of the light
they say we should just get on with it
they say protect your strength
because there are n o organs in language
no organ s in death
the event is so mewhere else
it is at the bent-over edge of the image
falling out of th e picture plane
peeing out in the sun
tinkling a b rightness

A ship, a loom, a dancehall, wings
the word for three
the word for lake
truthfulness and softness
arena, autumn, belt, ceremony market, person, satellite, quince
these are Etruscan
beneath the continuity of received gestures
is the gaping site of lost gestures
all else is s peculation.

/ /

Citizens of the library
I'm not sure, I'm no t sure, I'm not sure
I m iss
the smooth ind ulgent gliding
in the sensatio n of pastness
there is freedom on the skin sometimes
though som etimes not

now all knowl edge is a tree
inaccessib le to sight
any material's intelligence comes out smelling like ink
I think the dead are wi th us in our marrow
I thrust my face into the peony a nd I cannot believe that I am not a
flo wer

If language l oses glamour
we do n't live.
What is a school.

Most of what we h ave can't be burned.

/ /

I wore a dress of thou ght-coloured velvet
a little worr y-toned top
to embrace a 7 th century error

From Poitiers by tr ain to Angoulême
I listened to time
all folded a nd pooled
kimo no-like
all things pleased me
here there were m any rosebushes
therefore haruspica tion of rosebushes
plea ched
this trellis my l ined notebook
in air cool and exqu isite and impersonal
to affirm the active presence o f the future in the rosebush
in curren t living
contradicto ry and true

fair an   d fine
humble a   nd frank.

/ /

Frankly any w   oman's exiled
she's exile or   immigrant
bent over to dri   nk and admire
bent over r   ime that is
mirrori   ng water
echoi   ng air
stud   ying
the long survival of   classicism in Africa
from which hum   anism (medieval)
was to draw   its strength
I'm feeling myse   lf as its character
my small breasts pendul   ous over the round table
my feet in f   lat sandals
my dog at re   st in weeds
flies con   verging
in the glass o   f sweet wine.
Geometry   isn't dead.
The entire European tradition   of spontaneous introspection
bends over th   e round table
as my littl   e breasts
I suddenly sense with   a clear truthfulness
nothing is lost   or abandoned.

/ /

With language we sip th   e lost memories of others
and they open   up in our minds
the sentence that   I wanted to recall

was that the s   ound of the sea
has become absorbed by an en   gine in the ambient recording
I did not recognize what   sort of engine or its use.

What is not d   ocumented?
15 years of sex to arrive at   the beginning of thought
my thoughts do   not belong to me
and I   am free
to visit t   he poem
all my work already exists   and I simply borrow from it
Averroes says   the eye is water
the possible intellect   is unique and separate
we vi   sit it
and in the supr   a-sensual union
my study is ju   st beginning
my style is jus   t beginning
its permane   nt invention
is histor   ical work
we are in   the house
the lost   house.

/ /

Truly I am thinking a   ll the time about poetry
I am wondering about A   gamben's tone of certainty
but poetry really is the b   eginning of living together
the essential joy of spe   ech as absolute proximity
and inexha   ustible fineness
I want a suit the colou   r of the cloth of literature
dull-re   d desire
at the end of five   centuries of rime.
Rime is not wor   n out but recut
with casualness and s   implicity it comes back

where snow   is very rare
it sn   owed
there are   no unities
just this long season o   f the coincidence of
hazelnuts an   d cyclamen.

When I think of the scent of   ancient philosophy I salivate
I'm in it f   or the risk
but I have long s   pells of cowardice.

Most often, when it cam   e to the edifice of history
women were h   istory's outlaws
whoever knew w   hat they thought?
It moved unrepresente   d at the borders of form
perhaps their gestures rem   ained unrecognized as such
like their mora   l resplendence
I inherit thi   s question
the material   of attention
is gr   eedy.

A man herds a pig acr   oss a highway overpass
somewhere   near Puy
if form is not carried   across into translation
where does it   s action reside?
in greedy mor   nings of study
as five bright   planets align
there is imperm   anent happiness
a fire is   burning
I have lost all   my questions.

In this one perfectly beauti   ful place all the sentences
keep drifting awa   y and dissolving
each one of   them is a life

all the things that people   don't say live at the horizon
the greenness could sc   arcely be more complex
no style is fully   present to itself
they are little sea   scapes or forests.

/ /

The day I cried for Baudelai   re I had been drinking a little
the discovery that th   ere is no orthodoxy –
it took place in wh   ich hotel room?
I no longer unde   rstood my face
I did not then know that t   he metaphysical stamina
which I then discov   ered that I possessed
would become my   dearest possession.
I was ambitious a   nd tired. I began
with the assumption that th   e work was already complete
so anything coul   d be added to it.
Black ink shall be us   ed on white paper
blue ink sh   all be used
violet ink shall be u   sed on ivory paper
also dul   l pencil
eternal sadness regarding lo   st grand unfinished projects
their belated discovery – this   shall be flaunted inexpertly
I could almost hear the ping of   moths against the streetlamps
near the public garden.   Now the public garden
takes the form o   f everyone's kiss.

Neo-Liberal ideals are   completely non-erotic.

/ /

The fullest desire I can i   magine sways in the light
I am asked to think about s   omething that doesn't exist

the time in the descri ption splashes upward
in a continu ous ceremony
you must swe eten your liver
by meditating on a f leck of what's bitter
the art of no t perishing
is a t hrill.

/ /

Three crows
pluck out the eyes of capital:
whoever isn't terri fied isn't listening.

/ /

How a woman knows how to listen the world
depe nds on
an overview of the research as perceived from the edge of
sle ep
this is self -knowledge
I think of the time death appeared one morning
in the bachel or apartment
near the bridge
I wa s 26

I needed to dra w into myself
the experience of time at the edges of rooms
disappeari ng as I entered
in order to see th ose rooms again
their mort al density
I must forget everything
simultaneously evo king and dismissing

the supposed fe mininity of time
maybe I wa s desireless.

By making myself in to an image of time
according to the cultur e's self-consciousness
according to my idleness
a quorum of pr oblems ripened
half-visionary half-spurious
as Madame Blavatsky
the room produced images but they did not yet coalesce
my heart became c apable of all forms
I wanted to be a co-inhabita nt of the possible language.

/ /

Possible tin hut with b lue plastic rain barrel
copious tree-top of hard green peaches
moss-clad corrugate d asbestos shed roof
rain-blackened cinderblock of the dead neighbour's workshop
dense grove of river-bamboo
my piffling, squand ering disputation

Finds a snag in t he present tense
the spokes of thinking itch
make in m e a silence
that glows like a lamp
like a b ad taste

It is still on ly morning
in my concept of p hilosophical style
and I feel in my self the shimmer
of unwilling but h abitual submission
a little bit like love

a little bit   like god.
Here I   was in
the idle pleasure   of turning pages
lightly skimming r   ather than reading
here I   was as

Noisy fragile   and ghostly
berry glutte   d sub-song
the blackbir   d invisible
the songs are berry-gorge   d and are not servitude
I'll prove no   thing else

Everything I know abou   t the blackbird is this:
(maybe waiting is the onl   y method that isn't false)
a blackbird sings for 21   seconds of each minute
there are 5.4 m   onths of song
169 days in s   ong season
137 days of ab   undant song
there is presenc   e in expression
brutal and lusty and o   f elastic conventions
improvisation   is one tangent
repetition   is another

Between intuit   tion and habit
between birds   and their Latin
between putting out bir   dseed and pulling thistles
here   I am
one who fin   ds happiness
diffi   cult

We think we know   about kitchen tables
but we know nothin   g about kitchen tables
how will it be possi   ble to make a politics

free of all   legitimacy
we live abun   dantly and die
between neutr   ality and chaos
there is the mur   mur of notetaking.

/ /

March was ending an   d April was beginning
everything kept crawlin   g into the hole of a flower
in order for it   to be in time
because it l   oves poetry
which does not acco   rd with popular taste

I contrive to almost   forget even rime
in order to   be received
to be i   n time
I only hav   e to repeat
prosa   ically
who gathe   rs the wind
who hoard   s the wind
who reaps   the wind
the wind s   o belated
as to be   defunct
since   1209
there is n   ot poetry
there's a nostalgia for a mo   ment in which poetry was real
o   r
Brief time of the   poem is very long
to the extent that   it loses its identity
in relation to   an exclusion
and forever swims   against the current
poetry is exce   ptional quotation
we don't leave be   hind our condition.

It was May again, mau vish, the Spring of 2021
I s aid
I'll t hink
with twigs
how long do I get?
as a flower is a measure
the flowers so forcibly present
I will descr ibe flowers
which is to say the iris
the varieti es of edge
edge beco ming light

They do not waste the ir striving in duration
they have no good nor evil disposition
the fact of the dir ection of the iris
could mean something be tween duration and will

In the week when swal lows enter the house
the small v oice says
the soul hold s the warmth
like crus hed grass
where th e deer lay
before bounding o ff at my approach

Flowers draw th e light to earth
they have not av oided repetition
in the night th e iris is a soul
who weeps an d goes singing
you can cheat m e of everything
except th is song

sky-blue golden green-gr ey blue saffron amethyst
white-grey che stnut brown
pink yello w like wax
ir is

Through the iris the inani mate speaks to the animate
and the animate spe aks to the inanimate
when a person speaks t o her own intelligence
that is prose
and sometimes love spe aks like a human creature
and that is rime
it yields a greeting
it is plain witho ut being divided
I will not divide it
I do not divide. Love and the subtle heart are one thing
it might be divided
I make myse lf into two
with a spring- like firstness

Love's int elligence
is spe ech
some thin gs are free
but dif ficult
what if there is alr eady no freedom
now the sky is p utty coloured

Utter didact
outer didact
What can you say about the world?
it's a 365-day s ymposium
in my dream of indifference
to speak and shi ver and forget

is all I want
and the mist pouring into the yard at dawn.

/ /

Slowly and repeatedly fin ding geometry at dawn
we work with a mat ter that resists us
solitude magnifies
tendernes s is patient
we are each on the edg e of an invisible abyss
orange-brown an d bead-brilliant
over gree n variants
benea th mist

My strategy was to occ upy the site of shame
as verse does in the culture
snow on the branc hes and cold light
on the ancient three- fold division of love
within the com modious model
no other categor y no other twig
the conditions for t he liberation of love
were laid dow n by mystics
the sonnet is a political refuge
in it
we learn to temper resistance with desire
to temper desire with resistance
so neither disse mbles into force
moral abundance is as wide as rime
like this
my obscure you th was used up
assembling the dense st sensorium possible.

•

/ /

Every one of　us is exiled
mongrel cre　ature reason
mongre　l world
we have to b　e speakers
we still ne　ed to love

/ /

The bird is　my teacher.
I go to the w　oods to listen.
If I can't know joy　I don't want a world
what I ado　re I adorn
fully with the disc　omfort of duration
Cathars believed i　n metempsychosis
the circulation of souls bet　ween birds, animals, and men
ingenious firs　t motor repeats
new real equ　ivocal motor
in heretical e　rotic osmosis
I don't have the right to dou　bt until I have really sung.

On Sundays we rested in　the woods and talked
to make a little　bird of water
a dog of　water
was an eleme　ntal dream
we would go northwards an　d there would be islands
the earth wo　uld exhale
I practiced having d　ifferent thoughts
then I went to the c　ity to get things
a　s
downward-drooping goldy　-swagged delicious first
chrysant　hemum's

syntax of ungo vernability's
stammering flo pping pronoun.

/ /

Return now explicitly to the problem of beauty
which I had s et to the side
before 1848 Baudelaire s aid beauty was modern
after 1852 he said b eauty was imaginary
when the rev olution failed
what had belonged to the city could now reside only in the
per son
if the imaginat ion is personal
(now I thi nk it isn't)

One room passes th rough another room
there was a feeling of being held, as if weighted, on a sill
that I would never cross
all my effort poured into the wish to enter that
mysterious a nd desired place
I had a little bit of money an d a mistaken sense of freedom
I had my devotion
I thought it was rare
I wanted the wh ole world feeling
of a minimalis t nature movie
completed by a n avant-gardist
in 1 986

Bright g rey dawn
light covered us lightly like a sheet
a clearing ha ze drew back
I've been here b efore but haven't
to write novels about poetry might be the remaining task.

/ /

I couldn't arrive at an imag   e of how it would happen
              and then i   t happened
      and now it is behind   me but also I'm in it
           sea-like, far   out, floating
     I go to a clearing in   the woods to breathe
              breath k   nows her
       and her image acco   mpanies me as usual
  as her exemplary pleasu   re in the silky landscape
          with farouc   he perfumes

          Belt of stiff gr   ief and collar
            now my thr   oat is strict
         and there is n   o consolation
            a woma   n barks.

/ /

What's the little sill bet   ween speech and song?
        technology of   a gentle heresy
        whose sole int   ent is to widen
   the possibilities of   moral experience
        moral experi   ence of a dog
      moral experien   ce of a blackbird
       moral experie   nce of a robin
          be fabulous   and fierce
     for the dog, the bl   ackbird, the robin
  there's a clicking sound   from the upper foliage
   and the presence of   what's ungrievable.

/ /

Berry gatherers an　d snail gatherers
their future is modelled on the　irregularity of the present
her pail a moon　of white plastic

She wakes up an　d she's a flower
she doesn'　t wake up
the earth　is hungry
she wakes up an　d she's a flower
she doesn'　t wake up
the arts of peace a　re unrecognized
but inventive ev　en in dormancy
rime does not contrac　t she does not extract
the landscape of the inv　isible becomes visible
I decide in the dream that　I can be dead and alive
at the sa　me time
which seems t　o be the case

In what sense do　es she cohere?
as day c　oheres
she is d　ay now
although she's b　eneath the earth
in rime　that is
her entire b　ody glances
then the s　ky deepens
dimly glea　ming indigo
the lights aga　inst it brighter
the trees　blacker.

/ /

In the fable of the robin and the fox
they don't know why females sing
this real object wor ks as a foldable object
like the shadowy doo r in a Courbet painting
behind the abse nt Jeanne Duval
she has taken the do or to leave the image

A door was standing open in the image, exposing the poem
I've used up my prose now
the sheet is l ightly creased
like a sea movi ng over my body
like an impu re repetition
everything will be the sam e without being identical
I'll be the feminine man whos e joy resists all appropriation
I'll include the ide a of untimeliness
though the narrati ve is built of time
time being the te chnical material
this the end of the oli ve-green notebook.

/ /

Now in the embos sed cloth notebook
my thing-lik e resistance
is neither usef ul nor useless
so it is lik e desire –
inhu man.
By page 8 the questio n of desire is dropped.
What happened bet ween 1966 and 1970?
Be careful. Careful now.
What is transmitted when t he cosmology is truncated?

A form lo   pped off.
Whatever can be transmitted   in a general context of force?

I feel the whole rush of my   my blond grandmother's life
pass through m   e in an instant
I'd like to make a legitimate   contribution to uncertainty
all around me are fa   bulous materials
in the distance I h   ear a consonant
I know that femininity is   to outlive one's worth
because I am obso   lete I can change

I have three hearts   and they are deer
they ar   e deer
hearts a   re deer
they are wearing   the heads of deer
I recognize them t   hrough the fence
we exist in perv   erse conditions
we wo   men
whatever w   omen are
or d   eer
now it is hard for m   e to say what I am
the f   act is
I would make each mistak   e again if I had the choice
it is a shocki   ng realization
complete   ly freeing
the doubling   is novelistic

To sit in a chair a   nd do nothing
sometimes to wr   ite a few words
as I observe m   y own decay
it is what   I prefer
now I think on   ly of distance
I wake   early

to watch the   mist burn off
it doesn'   t burn off
but settles   in the yard
as I putter a   nd plunder
on this earth   knit of nerves
this also   is comedy
politics is too li   miting a concept.

/ /

Now I withdraw from t   he limiting boulevards
although I do enjoy   them in a minute
every part of ti   me is this tree
I will become it   s conspirator
to enjoy the sensation of   my mind transforming
the greenness   of the world
keeps producing more gree   n, says Mónica de la Torre

I open my e   mpty hands
so my joy in   comparable
as a doe as br   ight as snow
as a hare s   hall riddle
the edge of   distraction
as a moth k   nows god
this is my   ambition

Every day I go to the sente   nce but yesterday I did not
I put my hands into my clot   thes and the earth goes still
inside the senten   ce there's a tree
there's a bird that whinni   es like a horse at dawn
one field breaks into o   r across another field
these days I a   m voracious
now I veer away from m   y beliefs about my body.

Face /

A man's muteness runs through this riot that is my sentence.

I am concerned here with the face and hands and snout.

All surfaces stream dark circumstance of utterance.

What can I escape?

Am I also trying to return?

Not the private bucket, not the 7,000 griefs in the bucket of each cold
  clammy word.

But just as strongly I willed myself toward this neutrality.

I have not loved enough or worked.

What I want to do here is infiltrate sincerity.

I must speak of what actually happens.

Could it be terrible then?

I find abstraction in monotony, only an object, falling.

Gradually the tree came to speak to me.

I heard two centuries of assonance, and then rhyme.

*Had I the choice again, I'd enter whole climates superbly indifferent to
  abstraction.*

I saw amazing systems that immediately buckled.

*Here I make delicate reference to the Italian goddess Cardea who shuts
  what is open and opens what is shut.*

I conceived of an organ slightly larger than skin, a structure of inhuman love minus nostalgia or time.

Honeysuckle, elder, moss, followed one another like a sequence of phrases in a sentence, distinct, yet contributing successively to an ambience that for the sake of convenience I will call the present.

I experienced a transitive sensation to the left of my mind.

I am concerned here with the face and hands and snout.

Was I a plunderer then?

I am interested in whatever mobilizes and rescues the body.

I saw the sentiment of my era, then published its correspondence.

I am satisfied with so little.

I felt pampered by the austerity – it pushed my hip so I rolled.

I become the person who walks through the door.

The air goes soft and I'm cushioned as by the skin of an animal.

I can only make a report.

Womanliness knows nothing and laughs.

I can't live for leaves, for grass, for animals.

All surfaces stream dark circumstance of utterance.

I can't say any of these words.

Gradually the tree comes to speak to me.

I collaborated with my boredom.

I write this ornament, yet I had not thought of time.

I come to you for information.

Sometimes I'm just solid with anger and I am certain I will die from it.

I conceived of an organ slightly larger than skin, a structure of inhuman love minus nostalgia or time.

If only I could achieve frankness.

I could be quiet enough to hear the culverts trickling.

I'm talking about weird morphing catalogues and fugitive glances.

I could have been wrong.

I subsist by these glances.

I desire nothing humble or abridged.

I'm using the words of humans to say what I want to know.

I did not sigh.

I confined my thievery to perishable items.

I do not want to speak partially.

I loosened across landscape.

I doubt that I am original.

I've been lucky and I'm thankful.

I dreamt I lied.

I stole butter and I studied love.

Something delighted me.

And if l am not cherished?

I endlessly close.

But just as strongly I willed myself toward this neutrality.

I enjoyed that pleasure I now inhabit.

I collaborated with my boredom.

I experienced a transitive sensation to the left of my mind.

I stood in the horizontal and vertical cultures of words like a bar in a graph.

I feel like the city itself should confess.

With the guilt that I quietly believe anything, I dreamt I lied.

I felt pampered by the austerity – it pushed my hip so I rolled.

I desire nothing humble or abridged.

I find abstraction in monotony, only an object, falling.

Yet I enjoyed sex in the shortening seasons.

I had at my disposal my feet and my lungs and these slimnesses.

I am satisfied with so little.

I had insisted on my body's joy and little else.

I wish not to judge or to dawdle.

I had no plan but to advance into Saturday.

I had a sense that I'd strengthen, and speak less.

It was a chic ideal.

Look, I'm stupid and desperate and florid with it.

I have an image of it.

Had I the choice again, I'd enter whole climates superbly indifferent to abstraction.

I have been like lyric.

I withdrew from all want and all knowledge.

I have myself defined the form and the vulnerability of this empiricism.

I heard that death is the work of vocables toward silence.

I have no complaints.

I could have been wrong.

I have not loved enough or worked.

I have myself defined the form and the vulnerability of this empiricism.

I have nothing to say.

I come to you for information.

I burn, I blurt, I am sure to forget.

In the evening I walked through the terrific solidity of fragrance, not memory.

I heard that death is the work of vocables toward silence.

Honeysuckle, elder, moss, followed one another like a sequence of
    phrases in a sentence, contributing successively to an ambience
    that for the sake of convenience I will call the present.

I heard two centuries of assonance, and then rhyme.

I may have been someone who was doing nothing more than studying
    the Norman flax bloom.

I let myself write these sentences.

I needed history in order to explain myself.

I loosened across landscape.

I raised my voice to say *No!*

I made my way to London.

I made my way to London.

I must speak of our poverty in the poem.

I can't live for leaves, for grass, for animals.

I must speak of what actually happens.

I'm a popstar and this is how I feel.

I only know one thing: I, who allots her fickle rights.

I feel like the city itself should confess.

I only wanted to live on apples, in a meadow, with quiet.

I can only make a report.

I permit myself to be led to the other room.

I have nothing to say, I burn, I blurt, I am sure to forget.

I preserved solitude as if it were a style.

I am ignorant, but I know.

I raised my voice to say No!

I was almost the absolute master.

I saw amazing systems that immediately buckled.

I enjoyed that pleasure I now inhabit.

I slept like these soft trees.

I'm wondering about the others, the dead I love.

I speak as if to you alone.

Am I also trying to return?

I stood in the horizontal and vertical cultures of words like a bar in a graph.

I can't say any of these words.

I subsist by these glances.

Still I don't know what memory is.

I think of it now as mine.

Here I make delicate reference to the Italian goddess Cardea who shuts what is open and opens what is shut.

I took part in large-scale erotic digressions.

The present has miscalculated me.

I want to mention the hammered fastenings in ordinary speech.

I want to mention the hammered fastenings in ordinary speech.

I was willing to suppose that there existed nothing really.

But what I want to do here is infiltrate sincerity.

I was wrong.

I'm for the flickering effect in vernaculars.

I will construct men or women.

I had insisted on my body's joy and little else.

I will not remember, only transcribe.

This is the first time I've really wanted to be accurate.

I will write about time, patience, compromise, weather, breakage.

I sleep like these soft trees in sleep are sweeping me.

I wish not to judge nor to dawdle.

I took part in large-scale erotic digressions.

I wished to think about all that was false.

I'm really this classical man.

I withdrew from all want and knowledge.

In the strange shops and streets I produce this sign of spoken
equilibrium.

I write this ornament, yet I had not thought of rhyme.

This is emotional truth.

I'm crying, Love me more.

Its landscapes are cemeteries.

I'm just a beam of light or something.

I know only one thing: I, who allots her fickle rights.

I'm using the words of humans to say what I want to know.

I did not sigh.

I'm wondering about the others, the dead I love.

I only wanted to live on apples, in a meadow, with quiet.

If only I could achieve frankness.

I had no plan but to advance into Saturday.

*In the evening I walked through the terrific solidity of fragrance, not
    memory.*

Life appeared quite close to me.

In the strange shops and streets I produce this sign of spoken equilibrium.

I could be quiet enough to hear the culverts trickling.

In the year of my physical perfection I took everything literally.

Still, the problem was not my problem.

It was the period in which ordinary things became possible.

I am interested in whatever mobilizes and rescues the body.

Life appeared quite close to me.

I will construct men or women.

Limbs, animals, utensils, stars.

I crave extension.

Look, I'm stupid and desperate and florid with it.

I do not want to speak partially.

My freedom was abridged.

I speak as if to you alone.

O, to quietly spend money.

I let myself write these sentences.

Of course later I will understand my misconceptions.

I doubt that I am original.

Sometimes I'm just solid with anger.

I have been like lyric.

Still I don't know what memory is.

I have a chic ideal.

Such is passivity.

I will not remember, only transcribe.

Of Mechanics in
Rousseau's Thought /

'The women' is itself not a content

It is an unwavering faith in the fictional

Because they don't exist

This work was made under the auspices of opulence

In incandescent occidental forest

In soft pale-green medium-sized notebook

    titled *Many Notes Toward an Essay on Girls, Girlhood*

In the coolness descending from trees at night

Mainly I wanted to traverse a failure

Then I wanted the phoneme to spread around me like a sea

I walked beside the absence of

Then one had encountered oneself by leaving

And this posed the basis of a rhythm

As for the theology of certainty

The wrongness is philosophical.

I've spoken about drunkenness, 1975, et cetera

Where the imagined houses the real

What is interesting?

Values are said.

1490, 1501, cosi vulgari, 1503, 1507, 1512, 1513, 1519, 1525, 1539, 1554

With cool specificity of window-light in northern climates

I wanted to make something free

The streets helped me see

How it is that I am soldiered

With political bestiality of each era

I forget it here

Prodigal and Ungrateful

Meet in the speaking likeness

They are observed for rhymes and contiguities

Here the element of time is foreshortened

Rousseau is sobbing out his innocence

By the staggered beds of geranium:

Scripted dissent

Citizen-nerves

Violet stems of thistles

Cement buildings unlit

Odours of hallways

Summer was something pulled out of them

Which, by attraction and radiation

Would embrace and strengthen fiction

To the event of some trees.

How does it feel on your skin?

Slow enough to be accurate

An edge fraying so as to become a chaos

Under full soft hot light

Neither vocabulary at the expense of the other

Here is the concept of a vanishing point

In the form of gold or intense blue

Gently mathematical

I cannot help but penetrate it

To swim in the religiosity of the comprehensible

But the voluptuousness does not appeal to me

Speaking, what was it?

I had a little kettle

I had a habit

I had a sister

A hard time

It was a place like this with several centuries of human death added to
    it

With small gaps in decorum

And with great opacity

    even erotic genuflection

    cancelling all that came before

A hormone is a pierced cell unwinding to the sound of tearing
    mousseline

The sun has eaten the material

Feminism enters the poem, death enters the poem, rhetoric enters the
    poem

Out of a sluice of my own making

Then it feels formally false

True and primitive, one at a time

The mouth swings up

With its seven pure, volute resemblances

The little gods are interlocutors

In the mental sensation of living

There are watered meadows in the bodies of thought

Mountains and clouds and paragraphs

Maybe I just needed to presume the freedom of skepticism

And then to immediately part from it

    the jaws speaking

    a pebbling sound

I wanted narrative to be

The proportion in her hair

Not a statement of type 'I am choking'

As an authorizing system

Compared to the encoded unbelievability of women

The river squirts, the thought becomes a chatter

Imitating Pound's *Propertius*

To make a lack of value

Unseen, unfelt, silent, and inflected

And by their fountains

Of hope and demotic ambit

Which glazed, flayed, succulent

Let slip some

Senses

The suppleness of these amusements

Beginning – middle – end

The Etruscan scrotum of clay beneath Perspex

The wrapped breasts of a hermaphrodite

Wished to anticipate

   – textile-like –

The padded wall

As loss

The wrongness is philosophical.

October's topmost wandy slim branch

Unsnarls the

Air versus what is

Public: the technology of habit

I awake into an original greediness

Into glossy persimmon-crested notebook called *Sylvine*

Into large creamy notebook with title *Precious Ego*

Into small blue-marbled notebook with powder-blue cotton spine

Bought in London, December, 1999

Glossy black notebook with red-ink-edged pages, water dampened

Into many sexes slowly pivoting like leaves

The Present /

You step from the bus into a sequencing tool that is moist and carries the scent of quince

You move among the eight banner-like elements and continue to the edges of either an object or a convention

And in Cascadia also

As in the first line of a nursery rhyme

Against cyclic hum of the heating apparatus

You're resinous with falsity

It's autumn

Which might be tent-scented or plank-scented

Their lands and goods, their budgets and gastronomy quicken

You want to enter into the humility of limitations

Coupled with exquisite excess

You walk in the green park at twilight

You read Lucretius to take yourself toward death, through streets and markets

In a discontinuous laboratory toward foreignness

You bring his prosody into your mouth

When you hear the sound of paper

C. Bergvall says space is doubt –

What emerges then?

Something cast in aluminum from a one-half-scale model of a freight shed

Intrication

The slight smudge of snow in the shadow of each haycock in the still-green field

The hotel of Europe. Its shutters.

Fields and woods oscillate as in Poussin

While the vote is against renewed empire, or capital temporarily

Each wants to tell about it but not necessarily in language

I overbled the notational systems in transcription

And my friend was dead

What is the rigour of that beauty we applaud

    secularly

At the simple vocal concert?

The otherworldly swan wearing silver and white passes on into current worldliness

The steeple-shaped water bottles ranged on the conference table seem unconditioned by environments

I had been dreaming of Sol LeWitt and similarity

In somebody's visual universe walking

In the sex of remembering

But I have not made a decision about how to advance into your familiarity

This trade has its mysteries like all the others

It is a labyrinth of intricable questions, unprofitable conventions, incredible delirium, where men and women dally in the sunshine, their clothes already old-fashioned

They can still produce sounds that are beyond their condition

Here is the absurdist tragical farcical twist

In order to enter I needed an identity

In identifying this figure of reversal

The vital and luminous project

Will measure itself against women

And this has seemed poetical

When it is the ordinary catastrophe

I will take the poem backwards to this mistake

I will take your rosy mouth backwards

It is my favourite mistake

This masquerade of transcription

Hands torn crisscrossed

As the medicinal scent rises from books

Like a boat floating above its shadow

Build here the soul of thread

Pluck here the ordinary doubleness

Like delicate men in positions of power

They want the mental idea of the perfect plant

They want the perfect plant also

And I am the person who sits beneath the tree, listening to Calliope, attended by luck

Like curiosity translated as society

At 6:30 a.m. it was heavily snowing

The hills not visible, everything blanketed

I watched a pilot boat go out

Into mildness and vowels

Into this great desire to see

Always a boat in the middleground

And in the foreground, the men's powerfully moulded torsos

Twisting and bending persons of the foreground in turmoil

Make livid a philosophy

But not under circumstances of their own choosing

In these persons we glimpse belief

Establishing the fact of perception

Its inherence in history

Now that philosophy is collapsing before our eyes

Our former movements are integrated into a fresh entity, into a
    freshened sensing

And once more I go screaming to sheer manifesto

Also called shape

In several ways, each pigmented and thing-like

In the use of hollow space, which has in it pure transitions

Calm and hostile and alien

In the chirring from the yard

And in the appropriation of falsity

The *She* is thrown headlong into transcendent things

She swims into splendidness

She bites into her invention and it runs down her face

In this way she is motility

This is different from saying language is volition

Someone stands and weeps in the glass telephone theatre

Someone sits and murmurs

This dog that swims in toxic Latin

Licks his Latin paws

This is the middle of my life

Bringing with me my skin

I go to the library

How will I recognize disorder?

Yesterday I felt knowledge in the afternoon

The alcohol relaxed my body, which made me feel pain

My whole life straddled distance

Who is so delicately silent

By accident, procrastination, debt

I sat in the material tumble of fact in a T-shirt

Say I'm a beautiful animal who has mastered laziness

In reddened clearing in the occidental forest

In the album

Purse of goddess clicking

I long to see how it will continue to behave

And I am walking in her garments

In rooms made of pollen and chance and noise

Toward the errors in humanism

To untwirl that life, puffed and riffled

In the old clothes market

In a tangible humbleness

Smelling of copper and shellac and solder

To the extremity of predication, decay

Among the 804 works, merely to sit in unfamiliar light

In a mauve-toned customized van

Called the Presidential Tiara

Out of belief comes

The yellow light of previous decades in a movie

With flag-iris and wild-rose overhanging

There exists an obsession with structures that dominate position

To produce a deep unease

A hencoop and a kennel

Of high-nosed dogs. Odour

Of sulfur emanating from

A dream of paradise

A Cuff /

It is always the wrong linguistic moment

So how can I speak of sex?

One's own places realism in doubt

But now I want only the discretion of realism

I can't say it any more clearly than this

Philosophers taught me a conversion narrative

How the 4 elements change into each other by flattering

I think of them or meet with them in reading

On Oct. 2 showing their vanity and falsehood

With the frontispiece of him in laurel-crown

The room runs to swags

And popular flower pornography

The house amplifies the trembling as if its inhabitants are lodged in
    an ear

To make something from what I am

From proximity, bitterness

Is just brutal

So I turned to syllables

And if I degenerate into style

It's because I love it very much

All week long

Like a first thing

Like a technique or a marriage

Where conditions are incomprehensible

Thus satisfying the narrative of the body

Intentionally tawdry and valueless

And this is a recurrent pleasure

Because it gushes it's painterly

So that I feel abstraction

Is an incomplete resistance:

There are explosions of innovation

Next a strange, gilded, and embalmed repose

A single leaf laid out the circumstances of its development

So I attended vegetation

Where ornament is always unfinished

And it was a purely melancholic ritual

A fragrance so unexpected emanated from the document

Only to give rise to the striated ruin

Some terrible object presented to it

Dispersed over all the parts

Which are like nature

Miming the human

Painting can be seen as a faltering of that gradient

If faltering begins the ordinary

Discontinuity, seepage, and the disobedient will

Sit in the familiar light

Of the person

Without being specifically summoned

The models, the furniture, the clothes are all real

I worked in the kitchen with the windows open

So I could hear you

And change broke my heart

Their hands are love and their faces are love and disturbance

What you see and hear in the present is emotion

We live beyond its limits

The body bandaged to make it more impermeable

Then folded again along the top in a deep cuff

It is 1881, it is Athens, it is Shelley's pyre, it is not his pyre it is his boat,
     it is commodious and utterly dark, it is the camera's movement
     blocked, it is a non-productive economy but it does not deny the
     socius, it thinks only for inconspicuousness, it is only the King, it
     hardly ever results from choice, it masks an entire incompatibility
     using cloth or cuisine, it needs some sort of sacrament or corro-
     sive, it makes its own use of an effacement, what if it is just angry

That we must honour

What they created

Is senseless

The familiarity of blockage

Is a robust house

And the hut lost and its gate lost

Even immerged in her luxurious embracements

On a voyage with Lucretius, Catullus, etc.

You breathe, she smokes, he paces

Listen. The poetical work

Neither forbids inexperienced sight

Nor forgets their own mouth

I fall between them

An implement in its place.

Structure is duty

And fades as such

By these indulgences I lived

In their nice diminutives

Living in it rang false

If females lick

Language, death, economy

Cold sky with flat grey stormclouds

The seaport at sunset

Tubes of yellow light

This suture is a form of will

Furthermore the paradise is only ever indexical

I do not in any way wish to escape

Above the flat roof of the warehouse called Modern Props

Half past five in the afternoon

I'm about to copy this out

Because of having refused to

Break with the tradition of myself

After the recorder is switched on and before I begin to speak

All privacy rubs on it

One thinks with plants and rags

With prepositional inadequacy

And improvised throat

One's strange bare body needs a party dress

Tyrant body

If it travels

Came into the room as a document

Now these rites have to become intelligible

And wet the shining Babylonian coverlet

It charms impotently like a dialect

Where all the leaves are an opera

Silky things with fringes flung on the furniture

A sort of clown of the feminine

With the head of a nocturnal bird

As an uneven survival

Uneven survival:

Another maudlin dialectic

Billowing skirt over modern corset

By which I am strengthened

With luminous modulation

And outside the window the beautiful socius

In labelled packages

With ship-grey trim

Then with a thorough exploration of those parameters

With instruments made from negation

In the assimilating person

In a pronoun that absorbs everything

We have laid in the vocables of the not-yet-feminine

For a whole sentence at a time I become

The world with its streets, interiors, railroad stations, restaurants,
    sportscars, and beaches

If only in some minor respect

Labour was meant to be extricated from these things

The philosophical project of happiness

Approached, pressed against, touched, motionless, in the sun

I wished to pass scrupulously through myself

With subtle stamina

The ceremonies took place

Not to be redeemed

They elaborate one another

A work acts out the severance

There exists a labour toward nothing

Nothing being some kind of sacrament or corrosive

12:30 p.m. Monday

At the beginning of a new series

Just after church bells

I am too slow without you

Neither public nor private but nearly invisible

Seen on a curved stairway from above

Repeated slowly and formally in a dream

Bathers went to and fro through this flower-lined passage

So I pass from institution to intuition

Feeling sad spiritual pressures on the left of my skull

The order seen one night

Lifts, swings onwards in winter light

As for us we are uncertain people

Exploiting mythology in dirty olden sea

To and fro through this flower-lined passage

I slipped across codes

Using rosethorns

To indicate an idea about embodiedness

By slowing down the causal interval

The idea of the indexical

Is pleasantly estranged, dissolved

In the memory of matter

Such as the beige buildings of anywhere

This is the erotic feeling of non-identity

Suddenly the horizon folds

The biggest problem with melancholy is that it is more detailed than
    the world

Now it has spoken in me to become what I will be

Then I would enter the discipline of failure

And at the same time to be disinterested

I think a melting bell is silence

I mean something like this

The world already differs

And astonishment has caused me shame

Whatever listening is to someone

    black stone in ruffled pocket

Let it be valued according to its weakness

To annul function

I made this for myself

For the size and yield of its fruit

Its surface of variability

And concision and resilience

We manipulate memory

To make things free

I say pricked through, but I also mean

An inflation of monochromy

As a skeptical technique

Which plays out its tensions and conflicts

As in Dürer's *Melencolia*

In a finely textured conundrum

I met with the resistance that

Seeing cleaves

This is to say that labour can move also toward the single blindness I
 love

What people do is passionate, seen, and dominated

Now I feel like I'm that person

Perceiving from a house in progress

To go to the room where life falters

Everything heavy and mortal

Plato, Plutarch, Macrobius, Lactanius, and others

Sleep in the capacious singular

I too am cautious

The soul-hormone

Turns the japonica dark

Between stability and volition

Full-blown in the first moments of waking

The action of the sounds comes clear

It's like this – the non-identity of servitude

    the part that makes its own use of an effacement

Won't ever be revealed

What did radio and the phonograph give

The turn of the phonograph

Could forget about government

All these times and devices

Of significant imprecision

How does the language receive us

It receives us like a surly host

By slow consumptions

Now we run our fingers

Quick and innocuous

In the proper order and sequence and from the beginning

Between the telling and distant objects

Because of my body

In the absence of a system

    it is both in ruins and still under construction

Utopia /

In the spring of 1979

Some images have meanings, and some have a change in soul, sex, or
century.

Rain buckles into my mouth.

If pressed to account for strangeness and resistance, I can't.

I'm speaking here for dogs and rusting ducts venting steam into rain.

I wanted to study the ground, the soft ruins of paper, and the rusting
things.

I discover a tenuous utopia made from steel, wooden chairs, glass,
stone, metal bed frames, tapestry, bones, prosthetic legs, hair, shirt
cuffs, nylon, plaster figurines, perfume bottles, and keys.

I am confusing art and decay.

Elsewhere, fiction is an activity like walking.

Any girl who reads is already a lost girl.

Women from a flat windswept settlement called Utopia focus on the
intricate life that exists there.

What I found beautiful slid between.

We die and become architecture.

The season called November addresses speech to us.

The crows are still cutting the sky in half with their freckling eastward
    wake.

The quiet revolutions of loneliness are a politics.

Some of us love its common and accidental beauty.

I take the spatial problem of heaven seriously.

I look up from my style.

How do people work and sleep?

At about midnight in autumn

The nightreading girls were thinking by their lamps.

The fleeing was into life.

It was the same world, the same garments, the same loose rain.

It was no longer the end of a season but the beginning.

Clean as a tree, a face waits for form.

At about four in the morning, that first day

Which is a surface?

What is the concept of transformation?

The intellect struggled to its stanza.

The earth spoke in figures.

Its pebbles and tropes and vertebrae withdrew.

I felt a willingness to enter righteous emotion.

I became willing to enter certainty.

Then after a month it was the month of July.

The soft dirt threw the pink light upward.

The danger of the infinite opened.

It was almost dawn in August.

A dog yipped in sorrow.

By early June, I lost speech.

What about the conceptualized trees?

What about the phosphorescent gender that took my strength away?

I arrived at the threshold but did not cross.

How odd it is to think that a broken pier laced by gulls and kneeling
into the foaming pull was once an empire.

It is late October.

The house is like sunlight.

Soft and mild emotions were interrupted by emotions that were eager,
hurrying, impetuous.

People are fragile and finite.

Is this an interesting thing? – to be 40, female, in the year 2001?

How simple it would be to speak together.

It was a Saturday evening.

Yes, the future, which is a sewing motion.

These are the inescapable vernaculars of the Mississauga nocturne.

The effect of the downflowing pattern of shade on the wall was liquid,
   so the wall became a slow fountain in afternoon.

Our fears opened inwards.

Must it be the future?

Yes, the future, which is a sewing motion.

Most decay is not picturesque.

For one day there is the sensation that Springtime is waiting for us to
   walk forward.

Everything follows from the sweet-acrid scent of pencils in June
   classrooms.

Every angel is fucking the seven arts.

Each leaf had achieved its vastness.

A young woman is seated on a kitchen chair, black wings spread out as
   if drying.

It was August and the night was hot.

What we were proposing already exists.

This is a history of sincerity.

The tree uses silence.

The three layers of air flood the sky.

My face is tilted upward.

I wanted language to be a vulnerable and exact instrument of glass, pressures, and chemicals.

It has provided us with a cry but explains nothing.

I understand passivity.

But what elegance is self-sufficient?

Before primrose and before aconite, after snowdrop, at bluebells, during jonquil, inextinguishably for fritillaria, I stumble in and in.

It began at three o'clock one October afternoon.

What was I to understand of it?

Its intent is mordant.

It's weak and it wants beauty.

It was here that I first observed this question of withheld arcadia.

It leans on the transparent balustrade.

It is a continuous astonishment.

It arrives at nothing but the rolling year.

It always means everything.

For instance, to do, to be, to suffer, to bark, to like, to crumble, to sit:
in each verb I've entertained ambition.

It was only half past eight, but the month was April.

With greeny pleasure I wrote.

This is the melodic contour of the cry of a kind of fruitdove.

People emerged.

My body became apparition in the hot, thin air.

I wrote a story of beginnings, of beginnings, of meat, of words.

I wanted to realize failure as a form of tactile thought.

I intended to be nourished.

Because of the signals communicating from the fluorescent cavity
of the chest, because of the vaults of touch, because of the feral
knowledge moulded by the lips, because of the nearness to armies,
because of smallness

I intended to be nourished.

And then we went visiting.

It was the spring of my thirty-fifth year.

Since there was no solitary and free space I made one with my own
boredom.

I saw that the religiosity of the comprehensible comprised one strand.

Seeing is so inexperienced.

It's not my job to worry about futurity.

I'm on the inside of anything I can imagine.

I wanted to distribute the present, not secure the future.

What could I say that was lasting?

The smell of sex on my fingers was your sex.

Terminological difficulties arose.

That fine day our sunning species was so colourful from the little
island to which I had swum.

I can but equal them.

It was summer, a hot day.

Who painted the heavy rose?

We devote one of our meetings to love, an elaborate and intact theory.

There are all kinds of experimental protocols.

Tell me if you haven't had grief, a kind of gulped anger or strange
   freedom.

It could only ever be transcription.

I would like to enter a bookshop for the coolness and rustle.

I am ordinary and sometimes frightened.

Clouds are really beginning to exist for me.

Always I think I shall save the idea for the future, when I do not.

When will we go to reason?

When did they cease to be rooms?

Twilight is like mercury on queer moss.

The day in the rooms passes.

I noticed the viscosity of dimness.

I felt my arms love.

A man is shouting into a civic silence – please help me, please.

A distant thin ribbon of cirrus ebbs into space.

It was very early in the morning.

Like radios, opiates, the groin's endless currency and surreptitious
   edge, buildings torn out of earth and forgotten

Light could be tasted, had an odour like a tin can.

Girlhood is a landscape.

Across the morning earth, the pangs of a dying economy.

It was 1993.

Yet everything that happened was real, that summer evening.

What's the difference between a behaviour and a game?

The world with its streets, interiors, railroad stations, restaurants, sportscars, and beaches gains access to surface.

It is not true, it shines from our faces.

In the hinge between these things, a resemblance appears.

I wanted narrative to be a picture of distances ringed in purple.

Then I wanted it to be electronic fields exempt from sentiment.

Then I wanted it to be the patient elaboration of my senses.

Both are mixtures of enigma and proof.

Beneath the culpable excesses, the whole process depended on this same problem of decay latent within my attention.

An absurdly dominant wakefulness structures the light.

A style creeps up the hills, it is not true either, but it is made from local materials.

On the second Monday of October, at ten minutes past eleven

I'm referring to the scrim upon which one scribbles the unaccountable, the pliable and monstrous inner rooms, the solitary shimmer of the video installation.

I was drunk on well-cut gabardine, jets, and failure.

I took literally everything that transpired.

About poverty and ambition:

The account was probably inaccurate.

On a Monday morning in June last summer

Weeds were accurate.

Trees, clouds, faces prognosticate.

These little spiritual boughs of movement hid the lyric.

The sun glitters on the top of the sycamore while the lower branches deepen to blue.

The sky is the organ of sentiment.

The opacity thickens to topology and backwards to rubbing.

Small foliage brushes the words.

Money is ordinary and truly vernal.

Intensities and climates pass over the face.

Form is not cruel.

I couldn't then reach my thoughts, or recognize the details of my
    subject: who the lover was, the distant tile walls of the public
    transportation facility.

I'm reminded that Hazlitt spelled browze with a zed.

In late afternoon haze, a fuzz over the distant office towers.

It was its own ruin, that and the ululations of trees.

It was more an undulation than an object, more a gesture than a
    weight.

It is me.

Life left through the mouth.

Pigment isn't absolute.

Pollen smears the windows.

The blackberry vines are Persian.

The boulder smells faintly of warm sugar.

The core of it fidgets, bleats lustrous polychromes.

The face moves across the human.

Form is not cruel.

The core of it fidgets, bleats lustrous polychromes.

It tastes faintly of warm sugar.

It was more an undulation than an object, more a gesture than a
    weight.

It was its own ruin, that and the ululations of trees.

It is me.

Gates shut and open.

Also, the tree uses silence.

The next morning, eight o'clock in the morning of June 24th, 1962

I attempted to picture precisely the scale of my homeplace: low buildings squashed or stretched beneath the swallowing sky.

Decay was foreshortened, the element of time removed, so that a building standing without walls was simultaneously beginning and ending.

Crisp slithering of dry leaves in August.

Clothes swish through the air.

Books guzzle the distance.

What about the great waxy hoax of the decline of heaven?

Traffic is the puritanical landscape.

Then the figures fall back into anonymity.

The valley ambassadors a largeness.

The thick black rubber lip of the hinged receptacle is the only obscenity.

The shelter of houses groans.

The fountains spurt nectar.

The creek makes a dip.

The contours are amazing.

The century specialized in a style of dress to accent the use of the mind.

The boat moves historically into a form.

Some nouns have five faces and so do gods.

So does the pelvis, slung with electrical apparatus.

People moving a one-tonne rose into a truck is communistic.

This year, late in November

People are fucking in the ruins of the recent past.

Mercurial botanies are swiftening.

Masses of women move in the distant street.

I had the body of a woman as far as the hips; below sprang the fore-parts of three dogs; my body ended in two curled fish tails.

I see this from a train.

I wanted to mould verbs from clacking fragments of justice.

Hilarity, spite, and tenderness mingled without quite losing their splendid morphology.

Here, namelessness is compatible with existence.

Here are pickets, a nut tree.

Girls chat in trees about the mystical value of happiness.

From time to time an 'I' appears among the scenery.

Everything is visible, barely disguised.

Clouds float, winds blow, birds fly.

On the left, the remains of a fallen female figure.

A girl stretches up to pick a fruit from a tree.

A city is always a lost city.

A pink city doesn't rise from the forest, but sometimes it does.

Two o'clock, four o'clock

By form I mean the soul of course, that crumpled socket, that splendid
   cosmetic.

Early in 1980

The unstable moving body's making pictures of behaviour.

You will recognize the impenetrable laurel as her home.

The description can't be reproduced.

Someone's history seemed sexy.

Place here a fifty-page description of errors made by the body.

People are flourishing inside all kinds of needs.

Just above a system, the slipping face is flawed and brave for no one.

It will always be sex for someone who will want it protected as sex.

It contains only space.

It has to do with light, the way light folds on things, the way light folds on my point of view.

I was timid in the visual, so I came to utterance – rhythm and subjectivity, that is.

Into dirt, into earth or whatever.

How do you tread in the world?

A man falls in love with a description of a portrait of a woman.

Whatever girl dares to read just one page is a lost girl, but she can't blame it on this book – she was already ruined.

The day shows a licked surface.

Splendid and slow, a waft of dark inwardness surrenders to a system.

There's nothing left to lose.

The day will wrinkle the bare tree, the orange bricks, the slightly different birds.

Quietly a shape becomes noticeable.

As I thought about these things, I watched through the train window the spongy ground with its buff weeds, the cold neutral sky, the fences of gnarled wire and glass, the empty trees with simplicities of branches, the coarse pebbly banks or cuts with their soft weeds.

Yet nothing was imitative.

Two o'clock, four o'clock

What still grows in Utopia's deer-fenced garden?

Tansy, thistle, foxglove, broom, and grasses shoulder high, some
    bent plum trees persevering, the pear tree chandeliering, geodesic
    components rusting in second-growth forest.

This is one part of the history of a girl's mind.

The unimaginably moist wind changed the scale of the morning.

Say the mind is not a point of origin, but a skin carrying sensation into
    the midst of objects.

Now it branches and forks and coalesces.

In the centre, the fire pit and log seat, a frieze of salal and foxglove,
    little cadmium berries.

At the periphery of the overgrown clearing, the skeleton of a reading
    chair decaying beneath plastic.

Palinode /

/

Though my object is history, not neutrality
I am prepared to adhere to neither extreme

That which can no longer be assumed in consciousness becomes
    insolvent
Because it doesn't finish I can be present

So I decide to speak of myself, having witnessed sound go out
Fear is not harmful, but illuminates the mouth

I am not qualified to comment on the origins of the shapes
The archive pivots on a complicity neither denial nor analysis can
    efface

It is not true, it shines from your face
Against the hot sun that hits us, nothing's peace

There really are no gods and goddesses moving in the soul
What is lost is not necessarily personal love

And pairs that cannot absorb one another in meaning effects
Go backward and forward and there is no place

It is not simply a case of the subject being dispersed in history
The smells, the sounds, the shapes are not meaning but are the city

This is the border – nothing further must happen
The spurious clacking of grass is a dry spell in thought but not abstract

Just as in dreams there is no limit to further over-determination
I do not wish to enter into that discussion

Memory's not praise or doubt
It is not a substitution, since there is no prior point

We were animals that wanted sun and luxury and why not.

/

Later, when I can no longer remain
On the porch, I will be passing over

The massy shapes of factories beside
The yellow river, the sheds on the roofs

Of the factories, the lean-tos flanking them
The loading bays and the stilted awnings

All corrugated, warming to rust at the rivets
It is not my purpose to resolve incomprehensible secrets

This is a song of no-knowledge
And this is not poetry

It is the King, scented like my body
But to want everything is not normal apparently

What we have not dreamed explains the visible
Let's not decide what danger is

Nothing else of the modest condition, not the damages and disgusts
And I feel no love among the civic troubles

The air is not quite deadened
I'm here in the not-yet feminine

There is no limit to its capacity, nothing that it shall not create
I do not in any way wish to escape

I'll be their glamorous thing then I won't
Nothing is more slippery or tenuous

It is not only about violence and use and their avoidance
Their communication is not only networks of dominance

Sometimes the meaning cannot be achieved by the body not by an
    intellectual effort

So what if I am thick and stupid behind my life; it is not private

It never quite happens
Nothing was abstract yet everything was absent

But this was not the city of melancholy
And today I am not political

There is no sea and no forest and no boat passing
In a way I am content to think about nothing

In simple despair we accommodate what we cannot control
Nowhere shall I deliberately deviate

Nothing other than this dissimulation and disquiet
Nothing grand nor classifiable, nothing secured

The crime is not incomprehension but refusal
I have wanted a truth that is unavailable.

/

I had undergone an influence of
Death, which was itself imprinted

On some moving sequin, the breath sequins
Heartbeat sequins, the organs and their slowing

Articulations sequins, which as they move
From the foreground appear to dim, since

They go out to illuminate
Some event so distant we will never

Know the instant of its perception
As if poverty did not have an abiding insight into the nature of
    insurrection

Borders and organs end but don't change
Error is not harmful to art

It should by no means imitate either the wilfulness or the wildness of
    nature but should look like a thing
Like free and unfree went walking

To the unseen city of antiquity.

/

Not to be ungrateful to the great middledictions of concupiscence
But 'the women' is itself not a content

It is not real, it is a communal perceiving rapture
If I am not required to be present I can go further

It points to a means of perception I have not permitted myself
It is not so much a query as a form of belief

It is a structure in which truth is where the other is not

Someone has garlanded the lead Diana with camellias though I find
    none blooming
I believe I am never free of the beautiful woods.

/

At one p.m. we were confident; now we are not
Nothing is enough

It is not quite midsummer
Technique is emotion

Later, its nothing crumbled.

/

Landscapes are not eras; they never finish
Because it doesn't finish I can be present.

/

Our health was not good
In a particular place I could never use words

If I reason I am not the state's body
Nor is the body someone

It dreams no pronoun
No, not an elevation of any kind, nor any plan

Not even the happy closure
Something, like nothing, happens anywhere

And some never love
Hence they can never be omitted

In their clothing they are not the Kings I know
I realized I hadn't really begun

I seem to have no desires
Or my desire is not very beautiful

Not even midst rills and fritillaria
Not even my seven-fold will

Here are new enclosures without end
Perhaps this did not occur in a material sense.

/

The beloved ego in the plummy light is not reasonable
Onwards he coils without touch, and escapes

I do not verify their prognostics
Nothing can be discovered but acts

What will we disappear into if not the moral filigree of praise
Finally nothing but this omnidistant surface

The sense is not the fretful self-important introspection
It was a process of assimilation, not of influence

Sudden rains never last long
They are never to lose one another again

It follows that these falsified arousals did not motivate memory
But there existed no other theory

How to be happy, how not to die, to lie in bed and think
There is no other priority

Nor could I mint a newer silence
The silence cannot be done into English

There is no choice between historical and hidden meaning; both are
    present
Presence is not enough

It won't assist my conduct

It was no longer the end of a season
I had no alternative but to become a person.

/

I said to my King don't die
It meant I had no space inside me

How did they become fearless?
I am to ask a question where none exists

Such scenes admit no correction
Nothing stands between us

Now watered now liking now tending now only literate
This morning is not everything

Now rare and obsolete
It quotes the dream.

/

The garden is explicitly not walled
They are Kings or they are nothing at all

They spoke not of space but of tables beds wells facades
Utopia is negative, not punctual

I'm not done with myth yet
A form whose nowhere wrote

Physics is not so much the setting for the fate of the soul, it is the face
    of the soul
I report my loss to a slightly confused woman not used to the protocol

And I arrive at nothing bur the rolling year
The sky hasn't yet reached its full colour

I want to hold belief and dissonance in a cumulative structure that
    moves to no closure
This won't happen because of fear

These techniques are not an end in themselves, nor is continuity
The unseen city of antiquity becomes nothing less than a mediation
    between psyche and history

Not a cloud is to be seen.

/

Nor an orchard nor a single soul nor
A dog nor a leather purse nor subjection

Nor trivialization nor worthlessness
Nor apples nor stars when the festival

Of war unfurls from garden suburbs and
Decks the patios in grand coloured

Swags flipping upward in the breeze bringing
The shampoo scent of blossoms

It would be nice
To interfere with the accuracy of the world.

/

I don't want to correct features and dreams
The explanation is no more important than the rain

It marks the passing of a world I was not in
Sudden rains never last long

As for speech that does not have to be uttered
As for the sexual village and its motors

She smokes in her door
This becomes morning

To hear you breathing as I write
Thus the secular soul invents

The day won't be long
Only forms are found.

/

To try to remember anything about how to exist
In the inchoate institution of

If this is a dress

Nothing but the I am no longer aesthetical trope
As the steeple lightens.

/

To make a mould is a formal gesture of love
There are two ways in which it speaks

Form is not cruel
This by no means implies that it suspends the effects of war

I believe that the King remains the West
I'll go into a field with the cattle

To take a rest. I will break myself open
Become the animal in its grave of laurel

At the periphery of the invasions, the fires, the forests
An old man paces his vegetable plot.

The Tiny Notebooks of Night /

I'm thinking about the women who have no sense of being history
        who come to index history
                their inner echoing sensation of loneliness

Like the earliest Cathars breaking away from the church of capital
        (religious inverts, as Culley said of Maxine Gadd, who replied
                the divine manifests only at parties

Sometimes)
        the distance in this complex artifact
                which is their resistance

As the magnificent rain solves nothing.
        I remember that generalization
                like remembering reading Herodotus in the Cary translation

The weather fell across the pages themselves
        also across the mental image of the pages as I read them
                the wide margins and the sea-like monotony of typography

The worn dull green embossed cloth binding
        these things having to do with wooden ships
                cargoes of exiled women

The sound of the water and the warmth of the sun
        even on battlefields.
                What brings me to this address?

The mistakes I made about solitude
        won't change quickly.
                My dissatisfaction with evening

Is about the evening of everything.
        I fall asleep I lie awake there is a storm a war an agony
                poverty shivering in an old turquoise city

How much freedom can there be mentally
    I ask the night
        I ask Stacy, Peter, Etel

I would like the forest to witness
    what isn't trash
        to be a person in the roomy stillness

Love planes above the field
    it waits for itself
        its faces are feelers

The moon hangs above the green earth
    she is half-effaced
        in my space-like body

She rectifies and dilates
    the flexible medium of the soul
        in its puffy nimbus

That was three years ago. Now that field is sunflowers
    I thrust my arms upward into the dark tree
        the problem of night is a non-realized tapestry

Every minute is a starting point, like landscape
    like the instinct to go toward poorness
        when the sun sets behind the corrugated agricultural shed

I think that perhaps my great love
    will be that shitty field
        sprayed over with fungicide at night

I'm attracted to its tired honour
    I feel the restoration of desire
        a star in the core of my body

We hardly perceive a fraction of our living
    there was a new tenderness touching my cheek
        and then you died

People can live extravagantly like trees
    trees expand
        the future should be awkward, inelegant, and wrong

A vine around a thorn
    emotion and perception are so fucking underrated
        the moon is weird

Freely at midnight the women travellers at the hotel bars of these cities
    speak of death
        one says she is an Inuk shaman

A position received from her father.
    She touches grammar all over
        I say I'm psychic on airplanes

She says there is no real darkness
    that instability can be recognized as material
        like gathering wood from the shore. I say I gather rags

When I squatted to pee near the lighthouse
    I found tiny pungent wild strawberries just ripe
        near the rust metal

One bleached crab claw in the low tufty flowers.
    Wherever I tread
        is a strawberry

I think the theatre of the future
    is within the present linguistics'
        stuttering vulva

Passing the empty lit stadium in the megabus
    by exercise rooms in condos
        too close to the freeway

Then I stop noticing the spaces between the sentences
    and I am foliage swirling. The book is a mind
        I borrow from it

A raccoon with 4 cubs crosses the industrial park arterial highway at 4 a.m.
    temporary benevolent peripheries
        might look like this

Volatile dispersion.
    Fenn says to read Levinas
        and I want to violate my preferences

Beneath the luxury discourses
    in the apparitional early photographs
        sleep arrives as an image

Clattering with bangles of light
    the faces settle into their being of light
        as dogs wait on the shore for their people

Who are out in the boat.
    It can be clear or more clear
        when something dark comes over something already dark

Night after night in the cinema
    there is never silence
        never an empty room

The interpenetration of the dreams of co-sleepers
    makes night a vast plain
        hearts turn there like leaves

To hail the quince-like planets
    in their dark tree
        the half-breath of the 'yes'

The other half yours.
    I'm no longer sleeping.
        Cosmos is a dress.

Because time is impure, asymmetrically dispersed
    just for the fun of transience
        the polished domes of my nipples speak

In the small sylvine notebook
   the ink changes from blue to black
      between the pinewoods and the beach

Behind the hotel of Europe
   to exhaust the designation that fixes me
      in the abjection of privilege

Dwell all possible human arguments
   in the shape of a pyramid, a cube, a dodecahedron, a doughnut
      a small egg, and a lemon. A lamp shines above the fog

Coldness rushes out of the earth.
   I try to think about the spaciousness of poetry
      while the ancient theme of abduction in ships

Continues.
   Pedro Costa says that duration is the material that resists us
      Dürer said that no thought starts without a sustaining supper

Carrying nobody's weight on my back
   like anyone heavy with awe
      I walk past the zinnia-action

Falling forward like a psychic cascade.
   What is this burning part of speech?
      A poster for the lost event

Lit from above by gold leaves of poplar, light
   sliding so quickly and goldish
      I am lucky to be its accomplice

Boat, go –
   This is the beginning of Utopia
      Its material is time.

/

And if I become unintelligible to myself

Because of having refused to believe

I transcribe a substitution

Like the accidental folds of a scarf.

From these folds I make persons

Perfect marriage of accident and need.

And if I become unintelligible to myself

Because of having refused to need

I transcribe a substitution

To lose the unattainable.

Like the negligent fall of a scarf

Now I occupy the design.

NOTES

Boat is the accumulated record of a series of indexical readings of the sum of my quotidian notebooks. Now I have repeated this process three times: in 2001, 2009, and 2021. Each reading has resulted in a new publication, which contains the earlier records amidst newer ones. The current edition of this lengthening poem includes two new sections, 'The Hut' and 'The Tiny Notebooks of Night,' which select differently from the older notebook material, as well as from the past decade of newer notes.

Versions of the earlier poems were published in the book *R's Boat* (University of California Press), in the chapbooks *Rousseau's Boat* (Nomados), and *A Cuff* (Back Room), and in the journals *Chicago Review, Capilano Review, Pilot, Crayon, Veneer,* and *McSweeney's*. My thanks to the editors.

Much gratitude to friends who read and responded to drafts: Erín Moure, Alana Wilcox, Harriet Moore, and Kathy Slade, who also made the concrete poem for the cover of this book. Thanks to Ralph Kolewe for patiently and scrupulously editing the new manuscript with me. Kay Higgins made the centre seam in 'The Hut.' Crystal Sikma painstakingly translated it to the book. Jean-Philippe Antoine and I translated the Benveniste epigraph. The Rousseau and Bernstein epigraphs are my own translations.

I remain indebted to Alana Wilcox, who has welcomed and accompanied my various projects at Coach House since we first worked together in 2006. Alana's intellectual elegance, keen eye, and deeply knowledgeable commitment to literature, writers, and the culture of books in Canada continue to make Coach House Books my other home.

In memory of the poets Peter Culley, who during a walk in Cambridge in 1999 advised me that it was time for my middlevoice, and Etel Adnan, who died in Paris in November 2021, as I was completing this manuscript.

BOOKS BY LISA ROBERTSON

Poetry

Starlings
3 Summers
Cinema of the Present
R's Boat
Lisa Robertson's Magenta Soul Whip
The Men: A Lyric Book
The Weather
Debbie: An Epic
XEclogue
The Apothecary

Prose

Anemones: A Simone Weil Project
The Baudelaire Fractal
Nilling: Prose Essays
Revolution: A Reader (with Matthew Stadler)
Occasional Works and Seven Walks from the Office for Soft Architecture

Typeset in Arno and Pitch.

Printed at the Coach House on bpNichol Lane in Toronto, Ontario, on Zephyr An-
tique Laid paper, which was manufactured, acid-free, in Saint-Jérôme, Quebec, from
second-growth forests. This book was printed with vegetable-based ink on a 1973 Hei-
delberg KORD offset litho press. Its pages were folded on a Baumfolder, gathered by
hand, bound on a Sulby Auto-Minabinda, and trimmed on a Polar single-knife cutter.

Coach House is on the traditional territory of many nations, including the Mississaugas
of the Credit, the Anishnabeg, the Chippewa, the Haudenosaunee, and the Wendat
peoples, and is now home to many diverse First Nations, Inuit, and Métis peoples. We
acknowledge that Toronto is covered by Treaty 13 with the Mississaugas of the Credit.
We are grateful to live and work on this land.

Edited by Ralph Kolewe and Alana Wilcox
Cover design by Kathy Slade
Interior design by Crystal Sikma

Coach House Books
80 bpNichol Lane
Toronto ON M5S 3J4
Canada

416 979 2217
800 367 6360

mail@chbooks.com
www.chbooks.com